CANOEING

Mike Michaelson
and Keith Ray

Henry Regnery Company · Chicago

Library of Congress Cataloging in Publication Data

Michaelson, Mike.
    Canoeing.

    (An Outdoor encounter resourcebook)
    Includes index.
    1. Canoes and canoeing.   I. Ray, Keith, joint
author.   II. Title.
GV 783.M52   797.1'22   74-34135
ISBN 0-8092-8879-6
ISBN 0-8092-8878-8 pbk.

Published by Henry Regnery Company
              180 North Michigan Avenue
              Chicago, Illinois 60601
Manufactured in the United States of America
Library of Congress Catalog Card Number: 74-34135
International Standard Book Number: 0-8092-8879-6 (cloth)
                                   0-8092-8878-8 (paper)

Published simultaneously in Canada by
Fitzhenry & Whiteside Limited
150 Lesmill Road
Don Mills, Ontario M3B 2T5
Canada

Contents

Courtesy of Old Town Canoe Company, Old Town, Maine

I

Introduction

Long before the endless black ribbons of asphalt came to subdivide the North American countryside, travelers were journeying over an extensive network of highways. As highways go, these were neither slick nor fast, although there were moments of breathtaking speed. They were a meandering, unhurried way—often the only way—of getting from one place to another. But they were clean, quiet, and natural, and catered to one of man's oldest forms of transportation—the silent, nonpolluting canoe.

Most of these quiet, blue arteries exist still. And spurred by man's recent (and somewhat belated) ecological awareness, Americans by the thousands are becoming reacquainted with this ancient form of travel. Latest boating industry reports show as many as 65,000 canoes sold in a single year with sales volume climbing more than 40 percent annually. Canoe dealers are reporting order books filled for months ahead as more Americans discover this fascinating multi-faceted outdoor activity.

For canoeing lends itself to a variety of interests. It appeals to

1

the fisherman who can strap a canoe to the roof of his car and hie to some distant lake where the bass are biting; to the young couple planning its first wilderness adventure; to the family with young children who can paddle peacefully down some gently-flowing river, camping along its banks; to the paddler who would like to sail his canoe, too; to white-water canoeists challenging turbulent rapids; and to those who like to test their skills in competition. Whether paddling across a tranquil lake or making an exhilarating run down a rushing, wild-flowing river, there is no better way to experience the joys of nature than in the quiet, swift canoe.

Of all the qualities that latter-day canoeing has going for it—quiet operation, compatibility with the environment, ease of transportation, the relatively small capital investment—simplicity of operation seems to be the canoe's greatest appeal. And it is true that just about anyone can jump into a canoe and paddle off into the sunset, though steering a canoe in a straight line for an appreciable length of time is more difficult than it looks. But to add safety to enjoyability takes some knowledge of the nature of the canoe and more than a modicum of practice. However, even then canoeing is not a difficult art to master.

For those rank novices who cannot distinguish a thwart from a gunwale, canoes differ from other small boats in the following ways: They are usually pointed at both ends (some canoes are modified for use with an outboard motor), and traditionally motivated by paddle without help of oarlocks or any other fulcrum devices; they move in the *same* direction that the paddler faces.

The recreational canoe, as we know it, has a North American origin (although its name is derived from the Carib Indian word *kanu*, which described their seagoing dugouts). The North American ancestry of the canoe can be traced to the birchbark craft of the northeastern woodland Indian. Its slight draft enabled it to traverse shallow summer-draughted waterways, and its lightweight shell and rib construction rendered it portable enough to be carried around unnavigable water. It was swift-moving and, lacking a keel, eminently maneuverable through rapids and around rocks and other obstructions. Ideally suited to the vast network of waterways on this continent, the birchbark canoe was later adopted by French Canadian voyageurs and other non-Indian travelers, who paddled canoes on trips thousands of miles long.

A variation, equally North American, on the canoe is the sleek, low-slung kayak, which differs from the canoe in subtle points of design. (In general, kayaks have narrower hulls, less freeboard, are decked over, and are propelled with a double-bladed [a blade at each end of a single shaft] paddle.) The modern kayak is directly descended from the sealskin craft developed by Eskimos to meet their very special transportation needs. Eskimo survival depended upon the successful pursuit

A kayak negotiates a gate in a slalom race. (Courtesy Old Town Canoe Company, Old Town, Maine)

of seal, whale, and bear. They needed a craft with the agility and speed to maneuver effectively in the ice-obstructed waters of their hunting grounds, the strength to withstand high winds, strong tides and heavy seas, and lightweight construction for over-the-ice transportation. Thus was born the swift, seaworthy kayak.

The modern kayak sits so low in the water and has so little freeboard that a watertight deck and snug-fitting waterproof cockpit fitted with an antisplash device is essential to avoid swamping. The rider fits into his boat so snugly that he practically is wearing the kayak. And, indeed, a skilled paddler can flip his boat and right it again with a kind of underwater somersault maneuver—called the Eskimo roll—almost as if the craft were an extension of his body.

Today, people have a broad variety of canoes to choose from, depending on the kind of canoeing they will be doing and the waters in which they will be doing it. Generally speaking, "canoeing" can be broken down into the following broad divisions.

CRUISING

Cruising—steady all-purpose paddling—is the most common kind of canoeing. Whether a short Sunday afternoon jaunt on a nearby lake, an extended trek down 100 miles or more of river, or a camping vacation into a watery wilderness, cruises usually are undertaken in open canoes that offer the roomiest inboard space for hauling camping gear and supplies. On the other hand, extended trips in kayaks and closed canoes, always popular in Europe, are gaining more followers in North America. In this case, supplies and equipment often are carried on support rafts.

Cruising is done predominantly on flat water—calm rivers and lakes. However, even the most serene river often is interrupted with a few stretches of more rapid water. (Those inclined to stay dry can always portage.)

Cruising—paddling for enjoyment's sake—is the most common kind of canoeing. (Courtesy of Sawyer Canoe Company, Oscoda, Michigan)

For the sake of beginning cruisers, many canoe clubs sponsor trips over local waters for a weekend or longer. These usually involve overnight camping, campfire and other group activities and, sometimes, the running of rapids.

MARATHON RACING

Many cruising enthusiasts sooner or later graduate to marathon racing, which brings the excitement of competitive canoeing to basic downriver (nonwhite-water) paddling. These are races against the clock over courses varying in length from 10 to 30 miles with a usual average of about 20 miles. Canoe clubs, local chambers of commerce, park districts, service clubs, and other groups, too, sponsor such races, which range from small events with a handful of competitors to huge races. The marathon races held on Illinois's Fox and Des Plaines Rivers attract close to 1,000 canoes and double that number of paddlers (2 to a boat),

In this marathon canoe race, competitors will canoe downriver against the clock; courses are usually about 20 miles long. (Courtesy Sawyer Canoe Company, Oscoda, Michigan)

and as many as 75,000 spectators line the river banks of the 20-plus-mile courses. The races, usually for two-man open cruising canoes, often have separate classes for men, women, mixed couples, youths, man and boy teams—and, sometimes, special divisions for racing-hull canoes. Paddlers span the spectrum, from the near-novice recreational canoeist who enters for the challenge of completing the course—however many grueling hours it may take—to serious competitors who spend most of their spring and summer weekends at such events and measure their improvements in fractions of a second. Some races include events with cash prizes for professional competition (professionals are, of course, barred by Olympic rules from participating in amateur events).

WHITE-WATER PADDLING

White-water paddling—traversing rapids—is a form of

recreational paddling made to order for people who like challenges. Rapids can be a sport for the expert, demanding strong nerves and good judgment. But rapids also can provide exhilarating canoeing for the average paddler, as long as he or she sticks to water that does not overtax limited skills and conventional open craft.

Why do people tackle rapids? Because they are there. One thoughtful paddler, who belies his scholarly appearance by spending his weekends searching out the wildest water he can find, said, "There is such enormous satisfaction in knowing you can compete, not with another person, but with the challenge of the water. I think that's more difficult really. The high tension level when you're in wild water takes a lot out of you, but it's worth it to make a successful run. White-water paddlers aren't daredevils at all; they are people who enjoy solving problems."

Running a rapid is an exhilarating form of paddling, but it takes skill, knowledge of the water, and—an absolute must—personal flotation devices. (Courtesy Old Town Canoe Company, Old Town, Maine)

To help white-water canoeists determine the difficulty of rapids, there is an international rating system that designates rapids by degree of difficulty from class I (suitable for novices) to class VI (for experts only, definite hazard to life). For water rated class III and above, decked canoes or kayaks are recommended to avoid swamping. However, even rapids rated no higher than class II should be scouted from shore before an attempt is made to run them.

WHITE-WATER RACING

For even more exciting sport in decked canoes and kayaks, white-water paddlers compete against each other. There are two categories of competition—wild-water and slalom. Both make a thrilling spectator sport, as is evidenced by the interest generated by the televised white-water events at the 1972 Olympic games in Munich.

In wild-water competition, boats start at fixed time intervals and race down a river through a series of difficult rapids, attempting to complete the course in the lowest time. This down-river race is a test of strength and endurance, with a premium on the racer's ability to read the river and pick out the fastest course through rough water.

In the canoe slalom, as in its skiing counterpart, the paddler negotiates a series of strategically placed gates suspended over the river in a configuration that demands precise maneuvering. The gates are numbered and must be tackled in sequence—some bow first, others stern first. Scores are based on time, with penalties for touching poles or missing gates altogether. Serious competitors must train constantly for this event, which has led to year-round competition and the advent of the pool slalom—off-season competition through slalom courses set up in indoor swimming pools.

FLAT-WATER RACING

Flat-water races are straightaway sprints on a lake or lagoon where there is no current. In general, events are included for canoes and kayaks paddled by one to four persons. (A four-man kayak, incidentally, is able to generate enough paddling power to tow a water skier—if the skier has been towed to a planing position by a motor boat.) Flat-water races are held over a course of 500, 1,000, 5,000 or 10,000 meters, with divisions for juniors and seniors. Canoes in flat-water racing classes are paddled in a high kneeling position in which the paddler reaches the maximum paddle leverage possible.

Flat-water racing is featured at many regattas held around the country each year. Flat-water races also are a part of the Olympic games. The winning times at the 1972 Munich Olympic Games over the 1,000-meter course were 4:08.94 for the one-man canoe and 3:14.02 for the four-man kayak.

CANOE SAILING

Canoe sailing is a highly specialized kind of boating in which

Canoe sailing is a highly specialized form of canoeing. The device at the canoe's center acts similarly to the centerboard in a sailboat. (Courtesy Sportspal, Inc., Emlenton, Pennsylvania)

the boater may enjoy the best of two worlds. There are several classes of canoe sailing. The cruising class is nothing more than a conventional canoe fitted with a sail. Cruising canoes are equipped with a stowable mast and a small (about 40- to 45-square-foot) sail. They are designed primarily for paddling, but when a propitious breeze arises from the right direction, the paddler can raise the canvas and enjoy a pleasant assist from nature.

More specialized sailing canoes are also available. These are stock canoes, but fitted with a more advanced rig and 55 square feet of sail. The prima donna of this class is the sleek, fully decked sailing canoe, which can attain a speed of more than 15 knots. Usually 17 feet in length, these canoes are equipped with a hiking seat.

POLING

Poling, propelling with a pole rather than a paddle, is one of the earliest forms of canoe propulsion. To pole a canoe, one must disregard the dubious counsel offered to novice canoeists by well-intentioned canoe instructors not to stand up in a canoe. You can stand up in a canoe without losing your balance or your dignity, if you are sensitive to the craft's tippy nature. You must remember to keep your weight centered.

Traditionally, North American canoe polers have used poles made of ash or other hardwood and 12 to 14 feet in length. Today, flexible fiber glass poles are common and occasionally aluminum is used. One end of the pole is fitted with an iron shoe to help gain purchase on the river bottom—particularly on rocks, boulders and ledges. For poling in swampy land, poles are available with "duckbill" pole tips to keep them from sinking too deeply in the muck.

To pole a canoe, set the pole down on the riverbed and propel the boat forward by exerting hand-over-hand pressure on the pole until you run out of pole. Poling is not too difficult to master. In fact, a recent national poling champion had been initiated to the art only two months before the competition; however, he was very strong, which compensated for lack of traditional poling form.

Poling is useful in canoeing upstream, particularly in fast stretches of water that are too shallow and swift to paddle. Canoe polers also compete in races—over a course no longer than a football field; competitors are required to travel both upstream and downstream and to zigzag between buoys to prove their capacity to maneuver their craft.

The best way to decide what kind of canoeing is most personally appealing is to try out several, renting the equipment you need to do them properly. By the time novice paddlers have become committed to paddle or pole, calm or wild water, they will be able to make wise decisions concerning what kinds of canoe, paddle, and other equipment they want to own.

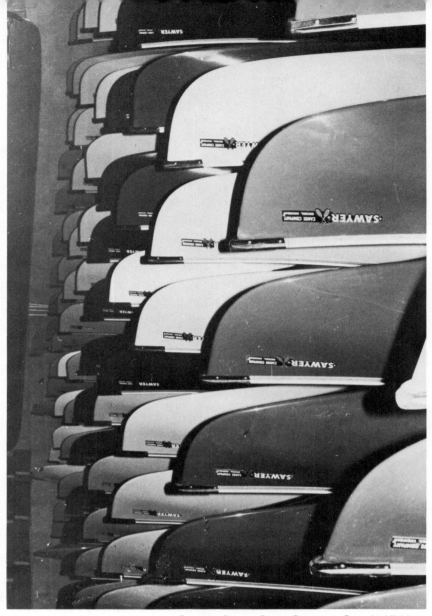

Courtesy Sawyer Canoe Company, Oscoda, Michigan

2

Choosing a Canoe

The 15-foot Alumacraft canoe has no equal in both capacity and stability," said an Ohio couple who had been using this particular boat for two years. Their decision to purchase was made, they told us, "after much experimenting with rental canoes and a great deal of trial and error." For them this boat *is* ideal. Since they have no children, 15 feet is a comfortable length, and their canoe's all-purpose design is suited to the leisurely camping and cruising on generally tranquil northern lakes that is the chief purpose to which their craft is put.

However, their Buckeye neighbors, students at Ohio State University, who prefer to challenge the white waters of western Pennsylvania and West Virginia on weekend respites from studies, have turned to more specialized craft. One, a highly skilled competitive racer, paddles the wild froth of rivers in the cockpit of a Lettmann Superstar Mark II from Hipp (High Performance Products), a C-1 decked canoe of the same design that won a gold medal at Muotathal, Switzerland, in the 1973 World Championships. Hipp builds a highly sophisticated line of white-water boats. The company has an exclusive license to

13

build and sell in the United States the designs of Europeans Toni Prijon and Klaus Lettmann, both former world champions whose designs have dominated international racing since the late 1960s.

The racer's friend, a more recent initiate into canoeing, has chosen a fiber glass touring kayak from the Sawyer Canoe Company. As a relative beginner, he appreciates the polyurethane foam flotation and the grab loops in bow and stern (all the better to grasp when dunked). Like Hipp, Sawyer makes championship boasts for its canoe designs, Ralph W. Sawyer himself having captured the "World's Championship Canoe Race" in Michigan eight times.

Undoubtedly, there are numerous other boats that would serve both the quiet-water cruisers and white-water paddlers equally well. And there is a vast range of boats to serve every stripe of paddler in between. Canoes differ in length, depth, construction material, weight, capacity, and performance. They also vary in respect to technicalities such as beam, rocker, tumble home, and possession of a keel. Which combination of characteristics you choose depends on what kind of canoeing you'll be doing, as well as your personal preferences. Discover what kind of canoeing most appeals to you and find out by talking with dealers and experienced canoeists what kind of canoe design best suits this purpose.

Except for a handful of giants, such as Old Town and Grumman, the canoe manufacturing industry is not large. There are fewer than 100 canoe manufacturers in the United States, and many canoe companies are more or less one-man operations. In other instances, canoe manufacturing is a sideline for a larger corporation whose main interest is in building and selling power boats; canoes are offered to maintain a complete competitive boating line.

Nevertheless, canoeists are spending an estimated $25 million on boats and accessories each year, and the rate of growth is climbing spectacularly, leaving many dealers with several months of back orders. And, as manufacturers frequently

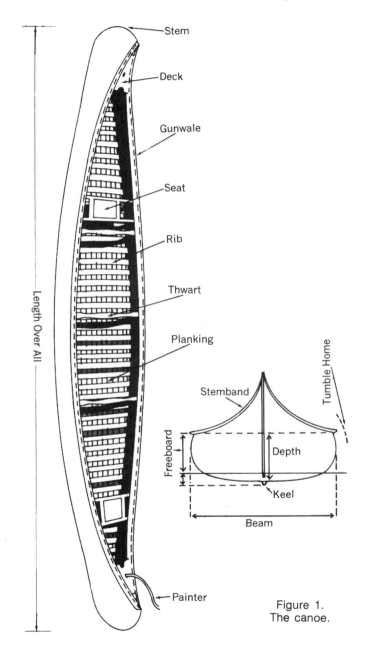

Figure 1.
The canoe.

offer many different canoe models, there are more than enough canoes from which to choose.

CONSTRUCTION MATERIAL

One of the first decisions a canoe buyer must make is what material he wants his canoe made of—aluminum, fiber glass, ABS, or wood. Each material has advantages and disadvantages.

Aluminum

Undoubtedly, the 17-foot aluminum canoe is the family station wagon of the paddling set. Many buyers prefer aluminum

An aluminum canoe. (Courtesy Springbok)

canoes for the same reason they buy aluminum siding—they are virtually maintenance-free. Dean Norman of Cleveland, a long-time canoeist and ardent conservationist, feels that aluminum is not only tough for the long run but also lighter for the same amount of carrying capacity. He also notes that aluminum canoes tend to have higher sides than their fiber glass counterparts; this extra freeboard can be welcome to canoeists running white water in an open canoe with a full load of camping gear.

"People who rent canoes that take a beating on rocky rivers," says Norman, "tell me the 17-foot Grumman, standard weight, shoe keel (see page 28), is the toughest canoe—the only one they can afford to buy and rent. However, an individual owner does not beat up a boat so much and can make other brands of aluminum canoes last a long time. I have used a 17-foot Alumacraft Quetico model for 10 years and thousands of miles and hit many rocks."

In addition to these advantages, well-constructed aluminum canoes are, on the average, somewhat cheaper than their fiber glass counterparts and cost much less than wood models. Also, in the past, aluminum canoes have been much less expensive to maintain, and, since aluminum canoe manufacturers invest heavily in equipment in comparison to some who fabricate with the newer materials, especially fiber glass, aluminum canoes tend to be more reliable. Though these savings still exist, the cost difference in maintenance of aluminum canoes and canoes made of new materials—fiber glass and ABS—is no longer so pronounced.

On the other hand, aluminum canoes are not the last word in modern canoeing. They do tend to acquire dents and kinks, will (unless painted) reflect the sun in a manner that is disconcerting to hunters and wildlife-stalking naturalists, and (unless etched and anodized) have a tendency to blacken hands and clothing. Other common complaints are that aluminum canoes are slow, noisy (multiplying the slightest sound like a backwoods echo chamber), and stick on rocks. They are also subject to failure of rivets and seams, which results in leakiness.

(A point to look for in buying an aluminum canoe is flush rivets. If they protrude, they are susceptible to shearing; also, protruding rivets inside may snag legs and clothing.)

If an aluminum canoe is the one for you, here are a few hints to help you get the most for your money. Make sure that the hull has been heat-treated. "It makes the metal harder and more durable," said Richard Pawlicki of Sea Nymph one day as he watched hulls being fed into an oven for a 9½-hour baking at 365°F. "Experienced canoe liveries just about insist upon it." Pawlicki also felt that the seams on aluminum canoes should be riveted rather than welded. "Welding heats metal to the melting point causing it to flow or fuse the material together. Welding softens the material close to the weld and probably causes the adjoining materials that are heated to become brittle." Canoe-rental people also feel that, regardless of the manufacturing process, aluminum canoes are softer during the first year of use. So, if you dodge the rocks during the first year of ownership, you'll be dodging dents as well.

Many manufacturers offer lightweight aluminum canoes, but this saving in weight is achieved at the expense of strength. Check the gauge of aluminum used in a canoe. A gauge of .032 generally is considered lightweight; standard weight canoes will run from .050 to .052 in thickness.

Fiber Glass

Some of the aluminum canoe's disadvantages are avoided in canoes made of fiber glass. For instance, fiber glass canoes tend to slide over rocks, springing away from them rather than clinging to them. This flexibility also can help keep you in the driver's seat when running shallow, white-water rivers. However, even if pierced, fiber glass hulls are easier to repair than aluminum hulls, though the addition of glass fiber reinforcement does result in a patched effect.

Fiber glass canoes are quieter and cooler than aluminum canoes, and a wider variety of hull designs—including faster designs—is available. Molded-in colors make them aesthetically

A fiber glass canoe. (Courtesy Whitewater Marine Products, Inc., Indianola, Iowa)

appealing. And engineering studies show strength-to-weight ratios higher for reinforced polyester fiber glass than for tempered aluminum. However, this difference is so slight as to be of little consequence in comparably well-made products.

One caution when shopping for a fiber glass canoe: In years past, many fiber glass canoes were designed to look sleek though actually they were weak. Unfortunately, it still is possible to come upon these models. However, there is no question about the enormous market for fiber glass canoes. Our survey results show some 50 companies selling a bewildering array of more than 200 different models.

ABS

The newest entry in the manufacturing materials lineup is acrylonitrile-butadiene-styrene, more commonly known as ABS. It is marketed under various trade names, such as Royalex, Cyoclack and others, and although it has not withstood the test of time that competitive materials have endured, manufacturers using ABS make strong claims for its superior qualities.

Ralph C. Frese, a noted authority on canoes and canoeing, reports that canoes made of ABS are tough, quiet, and cool. Molded-in color makes ABS canoes pretty, and the majority have a lot of flotation for safety. Also, they are relatively maintenance-free.

Frese notes, however, that not much is known about ABS canoes. Other products made of this material tend to fatigue crack. And good repair—even by the experts—is difficult. They also tend to hang up very easily on rocks and obstructions.

However, one outspoken boat builder, Whitewater Marine Products, Inc., insists that their ABS canoes can absorb greater impact than either aluminum or fiber glass and that even field repairs can be made easily with surface restored to original

A canoe made of ABS. (Courtesy Whitewater Marine Products, Inc., Indianola, Iowa)

beauty. The company also maintains that ABS generally is lighter than either aluminum or fiber glass.

Since there is little empirical data on which to base conclusions concerning the basic durability and impact resistance of ABS canoes, anyone considering buying one should survey available literature thoroughly and interview as many long-term ABS canoe owners as possible.

Wood-framed Canoes

For staunch traditionalists prepared to pay as much as two to three times the price of a canoe built from space-age materials, there is the wood-framed canoe—maybe even one custom-made to individual specifications.

"Quiet rides the wooden canoe," say those who would paddle no other craft. They choose wooden canoes because they are faster, quieter, cooler in hot weather and more beautiful than those made of modern materials. Also, wood-framed canoes are expressive of tradition. There are still a few dedicated craftsmen who spend many painstaking hours to produce a single canoe, taking pride in the use of traditional methods and natural materials.

Canvas is one of the traditional coverings for wood-framed canoes, but today alternative materials such as dacron and fiber glass-reinforced plastic are also used for skin. These newer materials seem to offer more resistance to cuts, abrasions, and tears than canvas. The Old Town line of "Trapper" canoes, for example, combines traditional wood design with fiber glass-reinforced plastic for extra durability. However, though manufacturers are willing to substitute plastic for canvas, they charge extra. Old Town, for instance, adds a substantial additional fee for this option on all models.

The problem with wood/canvas canoes is maintenance. They do not have as much resistance to bangs and abrasions as other canoes, and repair of rips in the skin and splits in the wooden ribs requires a skilled artisan. Varnishing is a regular chore and wood canoes don't hold up well when stored outside in inclement weather. If you must keep a wood canoe outside, try to raise it off the ground, and be sure to shelter it from the elements.

DESIGN ELEMENTS

Choice of construction material is not the only serious decision the potential canoe-owner has to make. Several design elements—length, width, depth, keel, and to a lesser extent rocker and tumble home—affect the capabilities of a particular canoe. A buyer must decide on the capacity, stability, and maneuverability he wants his craft to have. Since construction modifications that achieve one of these characteristics are made at the expense of the others, the canoeist must make compromises based on the kind of canoeing he will be doing most frequently.

Length

In general, the longer a canoe, the greater its stability, ease of paddling, capacity, and seaworthiness, and the less its maneuverability. Not only is a long canoe heavier and bulkier, which makes steering more difficult, but also it presents more surface for the wind to buffet, which can make it difficult to control in a stiff lake breeze. However, long canoes are quite safe. The most common choice among families is a 17-foot canoe; usually a family can pack along necessary gear and children without fear of exceeding a 17-foot canoe's stated carrying capacity. For single canoeists who are interested in white water, however, a shorter craft of suitable design might be better.

Depth

Freeboard—the distance between the waterline and the gunwales or top edges of the canoe—is another major consideration. Simply stated, the more freeboard, the less chance of shipping water—on the other hand, the more chance of being

Some canoes are made entirely of wood—frame and covering.

Canoes can be short or long. (Picture on the left courtesy Springbok)

affected by winds. Rapids runners should opt for high sides. Lake paddlers can afford to be less demanding in this respect, but a canoe with higher sides will be "drier" in heavy waves.

Beam

The wider a canoe—the greater its beam—the more stable it is; and if the width is accompanied by high sides, its capacity is increased as well. The increased bulk also increases its maneuverability in tandem but slows the craft considerably. And if the broadness of beam is carried well forward and aft, the canoe will go over waves rather than through them. Again, the compromise is personal and depends on what kind of canoeing you'll be doing most.

Some canoes are wide and others are narrow. (Picture on left courtesy Mad River Canoe, Waitsfield, Vermont)

Minor Design Elements

Three minor design elements—keel, rocker, and tumble home—also affect a canoe's performance although to a lesser degree—unless the canoeist is an experienced perfectionist.

"To keel or not to keel?" is becoming increasingly a question. Says Jim L. Rivers of Rivers & Gilman Moulded Products, Inc., manufacturers of Indian Brand Canoes: "The old wives' tales that a canoe should have a keel is a farce. To our knowledge we are the only manufacturer who does not recommend a keel (except for one very short model) . . . . A keel will be a hindrance for all stream and river canoeing, especially with a motor. A keel makes a canoe extremely hard to sideslip or turn. On a

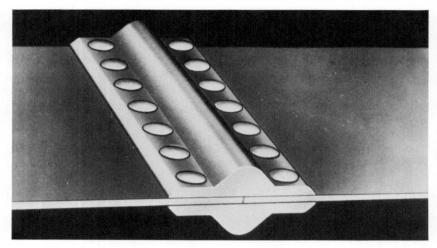

standard keel   shoe keel

A keel keeps a canoe from slipping sideways but cuts down on maneuverability. Some people opt for the shoe keel, which is a compromise. (Pictures courtesy Grumman Boats, Marathon, New York)

lake, canoeing with a keel does not allow your craft to roll in the trough, greatly increasing the chances of shipping water or swamping. . . . I myself, from personal experience, would never use a keeled canoe. The Indians never used keels.''

True, Jim, but the major buyers of canoes today are not Indians. Less sophisticated paddlers may value the added stiffness and strength a keel gives, plus its aid in directing the path of the canoe. On the other hand, as canoeists gain confidence and ability, they may opt for the greater maneuverability of a canoe without keel, which also has a shallower draft and slides over obstructions more easily. Confused canoeists may decide on a compromise, the shoe keel. This design protrudes less from the bottom of the canoe than a regular keel, minimizing the disadvantages of a keel, but still adding some strength and direction-giving aid.

A canoe's rocker is the degree of curvature between its center and two ends. Greater rocker means more strength and maneuverability but less ability to track straight and less stability. Also, it will not be so easy to steer. Increase in tumble home—the degree of inward curvature in the canoe's sides—also affects a canoe's capabilities. However, both rocker and tumble home are fine points of design, important to the average canoeist only so that he or she can avoid extremes.

OPTIONS

In addition to design decisions that must be made for every canoe, the purchaser has other options to consider. For Jekyll-Hyders who canoe and motor, canoes are available with square sterns to take a small motor. There are canoes with U-shaped

Figure 2.
Rocker is the degree of curvature between the center and ends of a canoe.

A modification of this canoe's stern makes mounting the small motor easier. (Courtesy Alumacraft Boat Company, St. Peter, Minnesota)

transoms to add buoyancy under the weight of a motor for canoeists who wish mostly to motor; and there are canoes with Y-shaped transoms, wide enough at the top to accommodate a motor but tapering to a well-defined point at the waterline, for canoeists who wish to paddle sometimes. Also, canoes especially modified for sailing can be purchased.

Just as there are beans and beans—pinto, soy, navy, lentil, green, yellow, brown, and black-eyed—so there are canoes and canoes—aluminum, fiber glass, ABS, wood and canvas, hand-made, mass-produced, sailing, white-water, touring, decked, open, etc. As we've said before, rent or borrow first, try as many different canoe models as you can, determine your needs, and then choose a canoe to fit them.

CANOE MANUFACTURERS

Aluminum Goods, Division of Alcan Canada Products, Ltd., 158 Sterling Road, Toronto 154, Ontario, Canada

Appleby Manufacturing Company, Box 591, Lebanon, Missouri 65536

Aqua Sport Canada, Ltee/Ltd., 525 Rue Champlain, Febreeville, Laval, Quebec, Canada

Baldwin Boat Company, Hoxie Hill Road, Orrington, Maine 04474

Black River Canoes, Box 327A, Route 301 South, LaGrange, Ohio 40050

Blue Hole Canoe Company, P.O. Box 274, Antioch, Tennessee 37013

Browning Marine, 900 Chesaning Street, St. Charles, Michigan 48655

Century Willamette Industries, 660 McKinley, Eugene, Oregon 97402

Chesnut Canoe Company, Ltd., Fredericton, New Brunswick, Canada

Clark Craft Industries, Ltd., 425 Glendale Avenue, St. Catharines, Ontario, Canada

Conots Cadorette Canoes, Inc., 320 12th Street, Grand Mere, Quebec, Canada

Core-craft (Bemidji Boat Company, Inc.), Box 249, Highway 2 West, Bemidji, Minnesota 56601

Craft Line Industries, 1880 Fruit Road, Algonac, Michigan 48001

Dauber Canoe & Kayak Headquarters, Upper River Road, Box 59, Washington Crossing, Pennsylvania 18977

Dedham Kayaks, Box 207, West Lynn, Massachusetts 01905

Delhi Manufacturing Corporation, Box 7, Delhi, Louisiana 71232

Dolphin Products, Inc., Wabasha, Minnesota 55981

Dolphin Sport Craft, 2306 Commonwealth, North Chicago, Illinois 60064

Easyrider F G Boat Co., 8822 SE 39th Street, Mercer Island, Washington 98040

Fiberglas Engineering (Oswego Canoes), Box 3, Wyoming, Minnesota 55092

Great Ski Manufacturing, Inc., 45 Water Street, Worcester, Massachusetts 01604

Grumman Boats, Marathon, New York 13803

Hauthaway Kayaks, 640 Boston Post Road, Weston, Massachusetts 02193

Herters, Inc., RR 1, Waseca, Minnesota 56093

Hipp High Performance Products, Inc., 25 Industrial Park Road, Hingham, Massachusetts 02043

Hunter Canoes, Outdoor World, Ltd., Box 189, Grimsby, Ontario, Canada

Indian Brand Canoes (Rivers & Gilman Moulded Products,

Inc.), P.O. Box 206, Hampden, Maine 04444

Indian River Canoe Manufacturing, 1525 Kings Court, Titusville, Florida 32780

Keewaydin (Vermont Tubbs, Inc.), 18 Elm Street, Wallingford, Vermont 05773

Lakeview Boat Company, Box 5595, Riverside, California 92507

Langford Canoe Company, RR 1, Baysville, Ontario, Canada

Lincoln Fiberglass, Inc., Route 62, Stow, Massachusetts 01775

Lowe Industries, Interstate 44, Lebanon, Missouri 65536

Mad River Canoe, P.O. Box 363, Spring Hill, Waitsfield, Vermont 05673

Michi-Craft Corporation, 19995 19 Mile Road, Big Rapids, Michigan 49307

Mirro Aluminum Company, Manitowoc, Wisconsin 54240

Mohawk Manufacturing Company, P.O. Box 668, Highway 427, Longwood, Florida 32750

Moise Cadorette, Inc., Main Street, St. Jean-Des-Piles, Quebec, Canada

Monark Boat Company, P.O. Box 210, Monticello, Arkansas 71655

Moore Canoes, Inc., P.O. Box 55342, Indianapolis, Indiana 46205

Old Town Canoe Company, Old Town, Maine 04468

Ouachita Marine & Industrial Corporation, 721 Main Street, Little Rock, Arkansas 72201

Perma Craft Canoes, Parkcraft Corporation, P.O. Box 315, Linwood, New Jersey 08221

Pine Tree Canoes, Ltd., Box 824, Orillia, Ontario, Canada L3V 6K8

Quapaw Canoe Company, 600 Newman Road, Miami, Oklahoma 74354

Radisson Canoes, Norcal Fabricators, Inc., P.O. Box 250, Callander, Ontario, Canada

Recreation Unlimited, P.O. Box 1024, Bend, Oregon 97701

Rich Line Canoes, Richland Manufacturing Company, P.O. Box 190, Richland, Missouri 65556

Riverside Fiberglass Canoe Company, P.O. Box 5595, Riverside California 92507

Royak, Inc., 3513-A Le Grande Boulevard, Sacramento, California 95823

Sawyer Canoe Company, 234 South State Street, Oscoda, Michigan 48750

Sea Nymph Boats, P.O. Box 298, Syracuse, Indiana 46567

Seda Products, P.O. Box 5509, Fullerton, California 92635

Smoker-Craft, New Paris, Indiana 46553

Sports Equipment, Inc., 10465 SR 44, Mantua, Ohio 44255

Sportspal, Inc., Drawer T, Emlenton, Pennsylvania 16373

Stowe Canoe Company, Inc., Stowe, Vermont 05672

Tailcraft, Box 323, Concordia, Kansas 66901

White Canoe Company, 156 South Water Street, Old Town, Maine 04468

Whitewater Marine Products, Inc., Indianola, Iowa 50125

Courtesy Springbok

3

Picking a Paddle

If you've ever been caught—up a river, creek, or anywhere else—without a paddle, you probably have learned to appreciate it as an item as vital to the canoeist as wheels to the motorist. It serves as both a drive shaft and steering mechanism, and it should be one of the beginning canoeist's first equipment acquisitions. And just as you always take along a spare tire for your auto, don't go canoeing without a spare paddle aboard. At least when you're caught unawares with a flat tire and no spare you can thumb a ride to the nearest service station. But when you're 30 miles and 6 portages back into the wilderness and your paddle breaks or is lost during a spill in rapids . . . well, you'd best start whittling.

Although canoe rental is a good idea, to give the novice canoeist the feel of a variety of boats, paddle rental is not necessarily beneficial. The paddles available at many boat liveries are heavy to handle and much abused. Also, cheap, mass-produced paddles frequently have little give to them. A paddle with a lively bend to it can save some aching muscles later by absorbing the shock which occurs to arms and shoulders when executing the paddling stroke. The canoeist plying a "dead," unyielding paddle will tire more rapidly. Test a paddle for springiness by putting the blade tip on the ground and exerting pressure on the shaft.

Since the paddle is not only vital to the canoeist's comfort but also to his steady progress in acquiring skills, early investment in a custom-built paddle may be a good idea. Just as in selecting a canoe, one must consider material and design in selecting a paddle.

PADDLE MATERIAL

An old canoeist's rallying cry, "Put the ash to 'er," indicates a traditional choice of paddle material. And though many paddles of fiber glass and aluminum are available, wooden paddles remain popular, particularly the lightweight laminates. Having chosen wood, the would-be paddler must then choose between hardwood and softwood. Each has specific uses.

Hardwood paddles are made mainly from ash or maple and sometimes from cherry. Both ash and maple are springy, but maple tends to be the sturdiest—and also the heaviest and the scarcest. Ash paddles are just as limber but usually lighter (a desirable quality on a long trek). Spruce is the softwood most used in paddles, although cedar and pine are used sometimes. Softwood paddles are lighter and, therefore, a good choice for children (as are some of the fiber glass and aluminum models). But they are brittle, give little, and break more easily. They also wear more rapidly, particularly in rapids and shallow water where repeated encounters with rocks, boulders, and the bottom fray the edge of the blades. However, softwood paddles custom-made with multipiece construction are sturdier than one-piece models and popular because of their light weight. Light paddles of great beauty can be made from cedar, but they are delicate and must be handled with great care.

If you forget your spare, incidentally, or break or lose two paddles, softwood is your best bet for that whittling job; and you might be heartened by an account, perhaps apocryphal, of an

Indian who felled a white birch and carved a paddle from it—all in 30 minutes.

In selecting a wooden paddle, make sure it is free of knots that may weaken it and that the grain runs evenly and lengthwise. (If the grain runs crosswise, you'll be paddle-shopping again soon.) In white-water canoeing, where brace and draw strokes subject a paddle to great stress, it is important to make sure that the paddle is not too narrow at the throat (where shaft meets blade), since this is the spot where many paddles snap. Also, beware of thick paint or heavy varnish that may be covering defects, and avoid cheap "outboard" paddles—cut from boards—with wide, thin shafts that snap easily.

Light weight and strength are combined in paddles made of fiber glass or tough plastic and attached to hollow aluminum shafts. High-quality laminates of hardwood and softwood have these same characteristics. These specialized paddles are frequently preferred by racers and white-water paddlers.

PADDLE DESIGN

Paddle design—shape, length, and width—is also subject to many variations. The short, rounded blade of the beavertail paddle, which takes medium-sized bites of water, is a popular all-purpose paddle. A wide, square-tipped blade of the paddle chosen frequently by racers, on the other hand, takes powerful (but more tiring) bites. Other traditional designs include the smaller-bladed, longer-shafted "voyageur" paddle, best suited to sternmen in paddling tandems, and the narrow-bladed Indian model, which moves comparatively little water but is less tiring.

Boiled down to basics, the question of blade width often is a matter of power versus conservation of energy. Generally speaking, for the average cruiser the blade should be between six and eight inches wide.

There are several different formulas for determining optimum paddle length. The Red Cross, for example, recommends

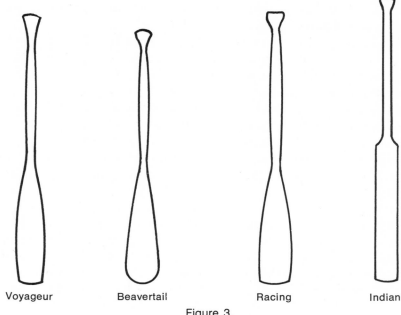

Voyageur   Beavertail   Racing   Indian

Figure 3.
Basic paddle shapes.

that, with the tip of the paddle resting on the ground, the grip should be at least at eye level. Another formula, using the same measuring method, suggests that the bow paddle come level with the canoeist's chin, while the sternman's paddle reach to his eyes or hairline. These yardsticks do not, however, take into account the height of the boat or the *seated* height of the paddler (discriminating, then, against short-legged paddlers).

One way out of this lengthy dilemma is suggested by Gail Cowart of the American Canoe Association, writing in his "Beginner's Workshop" column in *Canoe* magazine: "Length of paddle should be determined by its intended use. In most canoeing, the paddle shaft should be long enough so that when the blade is submerged in the forward stroke your hand on the grip is approximately at eye level (this being about as high as the arm can be raised comfortably for several hours of paddling). For maximum comfort, the hands should be spaced on the paddle shaft just a little wider than the shoulders. Of course, hand positions move as various strokes are used. If you plan to paddle a 15- or 17-foot boat alone, a longer paddle is necessary than if you will be sitting or kneeling with two people in the boat. Generally, the person in the bow can use a shorter paddle than the sternman." (The extra length recommended for a sternman's paddle is intended primarily to facilitate his role in steering.)

There are, also, several grip shapes from which to choose, although, basically, they are modifications of two essential patterns—the pear and the T. Choice of grip is largely a matter of personal preference. It is important, however, that the grip be comfortable and free from shoddy varnishing and blister-causing lumps. By all means, customize a paddle for your own comfort by fashioning contact points on the handle and smoothing them with sandpaper.

In a long day on the water, the average canoeist may swing his paddle into 16,000 strokes. But if a canoeist chooses his paddle carefully and uses it only as a paddle—not as a shovel, mallet, fish filleting board or tent pole—his paddle should last many years in spite of this statistic.

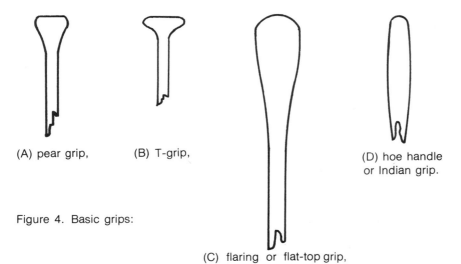

(A) pear grip,   (B) T-grip,   (D) hoe handle
                                                            or Indian grip.

Figure 4. Basic grips:

(C) flaring or flat-top grip,

BUYING GUIDE TO PADDLES

Alumacraft Boat Company, 305 West St. Julien Street, St. Peter, Minnesota 56082

Blue Hole Canoe Company, P.O. Box 274, Antioch, Tennessee 37013

Cannon Products, Inc., 2345 N.W. Eighth Avenue, P.O. Box 612, Faribault, Minnesota 55021

Raymond A. Dodge, 1625 Broadway, Niles, Michigan 49120 (authorized dealer for Clement and Nona paddles)

Hauthaway Kayaks, 640 Boston Post Road, Weston, Massachusetts 02193 (double-bladed paddles only)

Hipp High Performance Products, Inc., 25 Industrial Park Road, Hingham, Massachusetts 02043

Iliad, Inc., 170 Circuit Street, Norwell, Massachusetts 02061

Great Ski Manufacturing, Inc., 45 Water Street, Worcester, Massachusetts 01604 (single-bladed paddles only)

Grumman Boats, Marathon, New York 13803 (single-bladed paddles only)

Klepper Corporation, 35 Union Square West, New York, New York 10003

Lincoln Fiberglass, Inc., Route 62, Stow, Massachusetts 01775 (single-bladed paddles only)

Michi-Craft Corporation, 19995 19 Mile Road, Big Rapids, Michigan 49307 (single-bladed paddles only)

Norge Paddle Company, P.O. Box 77, Pine Grove Mills, Pennsylvania 16868

Old Town Canoe Company, Old Town, Maine 04468

Plasticrafts, Inc., 2800 Speer Boulevard, Denver, Colorado 80211

Ralph Sawyer, 8891 Rogue River Highway, Rogue River, Oregon 97537

Seda Products, P.O. Box 5509, Fullerton, California 92635

These early season paddlers depend on wet suits for protection against the paralysis that can result from a plunge in cold water.

4

Essential Extras

Like airplane pilots, there are no old bold canoeists. Man does not canoe by paddle alone. Good sense, followed in short order by good paddling skills and certain vital accessories must also accompany the canoeist on his quest for adventure.

Any equipment or clothing that helps keep canoeist and canoe comfortable and safe is essential. Items range in absolute necessity from personal flotation devices (PFDs), which are required by law, to the handy waterproof bag, which simply keeps the paddler's extra pair of socks dry.

PFDs

A reliable life jacket, now called a personal flotation device (PFD), should top the canoeist's list of necessities. Since October 1, 1973, the U.S. Coast Guard has required that canoes and kayaks carry a PFD for each person aboard. And though the regulation requires only that PFDs be available, it is best to wear them, even when training or simply cruising your favorite lake.

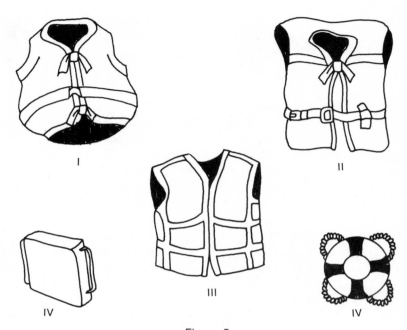

Figure 5.
There are four different kinds of personal flotation devices (PFDs) approved for recreational use by the U.S. Coast Guard (Types I-IV).

The Coast Guard has written specifications for five different basic types of PFDs, each designed to fulfill a particular purpose. Only four of these are of concern to recreational boaters, however. The fifth type is designed for use by people working in or around commercial vessels. Type I PFDs give 20 pounds of buoyancy and are designed to turn an unconscious person from a face down position to a face up position; they are recommended for offshore cruising. Type II PFDs, which also are designed to turn an unconscious person face up but have only 15.5 pounds of buoyancy, are recommended for cruising close to shore. Type III PFDs have 15.5 pounds of buoyancy but are designed only to keep a *conscious* person in a vertical position; they are recommended for use on lakes and boating very close to shore. (Type III PFDs do not offer such complete protection from drowning as do Types I and II, but they are more comfortable to wear.) Type IV PFDs, which must have 16.5 pounds of buoyancy, are designed to be thrown to someone in the water.

The American Canoe Association (ACA) recommends that canoeists choose PFDs from Types I-III. But canoeists should also carry one Type IV PFD for an unexpected man overboard, and craft over 16 feet in length are required to have one Type IV PFD on board under any circumstances.

Novice canoeists who are renting equipment should check their PFDs, as well as any other equipment they rent. Rental equipment is subjected to hard use and frequently does not get the tender loving care from the outfitter that it needs to stay in good condition. One New Jersey woman, widowed by a drowning accident, collected $70,000 from an outfitter whose flotation equipment failed to support two accident victims, one being the widow's husband. Although tragic, the incident may serve a twofold purpose: 1) to warn those who rent canoes that the equipment sometimes is not the best, and 2) to serve warning that outfitters have legal responsibilities to see that their equipment meets certain standards.

It is also important to shop as carefully for PFDs as you would for any other form of life insurance. Try out different types to determine which best suits your needs. Then check each brand for stability, reliability and maximum use in time of need.

WET SUITS

Canoeists are a crazy lot, paddling in the coldest weather. But they're not so crazy if they are protected by wet suits. It is difficult to comprehend without having experienced it, how swiftly cold water can sap the strength of even the healthiest body (see Chapter 6), and a muscle paralysis called hypothermia may strike inadequately protected canoeists. As we have experienced near paralysis from cold after a spill on Illinois's Des Plaines River, one of the tamest rivers imaginable, we cannot urge too strongly that paddlers wear a wet suit when canoeing in cold water if there is any danger of a spill. Though protective clothing—such as coveralls, thermal underwear, and good wool outer clothes—offers sufficient protection when the weather is cold if you don't go into the water, wearing a lot of heavy clothing can hamper your movement and weigh you down if you do. At that point, switch to a wet suit.

The number of wet suits available—and their accessories, such as booties, neoprene hoods, etc.—make an easy purchasing decision impossible. Survey the market to find good fit, sturdy materials, and moderate prices. Wet suits are made of neoprene, with nylon bonded to one or both sides of the garment for durability. Basically, boaters should look at wet suits made for surfers, as the ones designed for skin divers are too stiff.

Neoprene is also manufactured in two different ways, one of which produces a higher quality product. In gas-blown neoprene foam cells are of uniform size and distribution, which results in a more durable and better-fitting suit. The foam cells in chemically blown neoprene may be uneven in size and distribution, making chem-blown neoprene suits weaker and stiffer. Be sure to look beyond the brand name. Check the label and, if the manufacturing process isn't mentioned, ask the salesman. Or specify the type you want to purchase in the first place.

Incidentally, most diving stores don't carry the kind of wet suits canoeists need. But you can safely order by mail, because neoprene has good stretching characteristics and you probably can get a comfortable fit from sizes in stock. However, make sure the store will accept returns in case you *do* get a bad fit.

There is other equipment available, too, to keep you and the contents of your canoe dry and comfortable.

CANOE COVERINGS

One way to insure that, even if you get wet, you'll have a dry change of clothes is to cover your canoe. Covered canoes are especially favored by white-water paddlers, who are in danger of a wetting from spray and rambunctious waves. For the all-

Spray skirts, which fit snugly around the body and are attached to the canoe, work equally well with a rigid deck (top) or a canvas covering (bottom) to keep the canoe's inside dry. (Courtesy Old Town Canoe Company, Old Town, Maine)

purpose canoeist, detachable covers made of supple waterproof material give temporary protection in rainy weather, on a stretch of rapids or in the face of high lake waves. More avid white-water paddlers frequently resort to canoes with built-in rigid decks. Though very effective in keeping water outside the canoe, rigid decks result in decreased carrying capacity and inconvenience on extended trips; therefore, they are used almost exclusively by white-water devotees. Final protection from the random wave for canoeists and kayakers is provided by the skirt. This unique piece of equipment, worn around the waist and attached to the cockpit of canoe or kayak, keeps unexpected water outside the canoe.

WATERPROOF BAGS

Waterproof rubber bags, available in most surplus stores, keep everything dry—from sleeping bags to cosmetics. If you hanker for a custom-made job, Ms. Ann Dwyer, an enterprising Californian, is engaged in manufacturing these items. They are rather expensive—around $16-18 postpaid—but worthwhile. If you're interested, you can write to her for an illustrated brochure, including costs, at Canoe California, P.O. Box 61A, Kentfield, California 94904.

BAILERS

If the canoe does ship water, the canoeist has to ship it back out. Any empty container will do—coffee can, cooking pot, or, under trying circumstances, the paddler's own fedora. A tried-and-true design involves cutting the bottom from a plastic bleach bottle at an angle; the finished bailer conforms to the hull shape as you scoop.

However, canoeists can get fancy if they wish. Of the more sophisticated pumps, the hand-squeezed syphon pump and the battery-powered bilge pump are probably the most useful. However, the battery-powered pumps are heavy and tend to clog. Or a canoeist can have a "bailer" installed right in his

Waterproof bags are the best way to make sure that everything is dry upon arrival at your destination. (Courtesy Canoe California, Kentfield, California)

canoe. This clever device, first imported from Denmark in 1971, is little more than a hole in the bottom of the boat fitted with a valve so that water runs out but cannot get back in. It is gaining special favor in racing circles.

But no bailer is perfect, so be sure to carry a sponge to sop up the last drops of water from the canoe's floor.

OTHER EQUIPMENT

Kneeling Pads

Although kneeling pads can be found in almost any sporting goods store, a diligent canoeist can save some money by making his own from canvas money bags or old life preserver cushions.

Ready-made metal yoke

Fiberglass yoke with ensolite padding

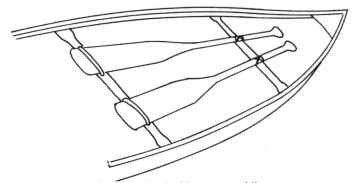

Yoke improvised with canoe paddles

Figure 6.
Three different kinds of carrying yokes to transport a canoe: ready-made metal yokes, which bolt over the canoe's center thwart; molded fiber glass yokes; and two paddles lashed to thwarts.

Carrying Yokes

The carrying yoke—a device used to carry a canoe on one's shoulders—is another piece of equipment that can be bought or made. Commercially made carrying yokes are available in hardwood and aluminum models and employ either fixed or adjustable straps to protect the shoulders from the weight of the upside-down canoe. They can be affixed to a canoe permanently or remain removable. The first requirement when purchasing a carrying yoke is proper fit. Also check durability of the

These two fishermen (dressed in Type II PFDs) are fishing in a canoe with a permanently attached carrying yoke.

screws or bolts; some canoeists have reported problems with wood screws pulling out from the crossarm.

However, carrying yokes, like kneeling pads, can be improvised. In canoes without a center thwart, paddles can be tied between forward and stern seats so that the shafts of the paddles rest on the carrier's shoulders, which should be padded. On canoes that do have a center thwart, the carrier should fasten the paddles to this thwart so that the paddle blades rest against his shoulders. Remember to plan for good balance and visibility while toting your boat.

ACCESSORY DIRECTORY

PFDs

Dauber Canoe & Kayak Headquarters, Upper River Road, Box 59, Washington Crossing, Pennsylvania 18977

Empress Corporation, 1144 South San Julian Street, Los Angeles, California 90015

Florida Cypress Gardens, Inc., Route 1, Box 656, Winter Haven, Florida 33880

Gentex Corporation, Carbondale, Pennsylvania 18407

Gladding Corporation, P.O. Box 260, Syracuse, New York 13201

Grumman Boats, Marathon, New York 13803

Hauthaway Kayaks, 640 Boston Post Road, Weston, Massachusetts 02193

Lincoln Fiberglass, Inc., Route 62, Stow, Massachusetts 01775

Midwest Outerwear, Inc., 603 North Moore Road, Port Washington, Wisconsin 53074

Old Town Canoe Company, Old Town, Maine 04468

Seda Products, P.O. Box 5509, Fullerton, California 92635

Sportspal, Inc., Drawer T, Emlenton, Pennsylvania 16373

Stearnes Manufacturing Company, St. Cloud, Minnesota 56301

Wellington Puritan Mills, Inc., P.O. Box 521, Madison, Georgia 30650

Wet Suits

Dive N' Surf, Inc., 504 North Broadway, Redondo Beach, California 90277

Harvey's, 11011 First Avenue South, Seattle, Washington 98168

Henderson Aquatic, Inc., Delsea Drive, Route 47, Port Elizabeth, New Jersey 08348

Old Town Canoe Company, Old Town, Maine 04468

Sea Suits, 825 West 18th Street, Costa Mesa, California 92627

Waterproof Bags

Ann Dwyer, Canoe California, Box 61A, Kentfield, California 94904

Courtesy Sears Roebuck and Company.

5

How to Paddle

A good paddle doesn't help the paddler much unless it is used properly. For a relaxed body at the end of a long canoe trip appropriate strokes must be properly executed. The paddling strokes that use the least amount of energy for the most forward motion are the ones to master. The pitch stroke, J-stroke, pry stroke, draw, sculling draw, and bracing, a relatively new technique, all have their place in the canoeist's repertoire.

PADDLING POSITION

Before even putting paddle to water, however, the canoeist must find a stable and comfortable paddling position. Kneeling is the traditionalist's way to paddle, and there are quite a few kneeling positions to choose among. Canoeists can kneel on both knees, at the same time leaning back against a thwart to take some of the strain off—and for relief stretching one leg out in front to prevent cramping. Another good relief position is the upright kneeling position in which the canoeist is actually stand-

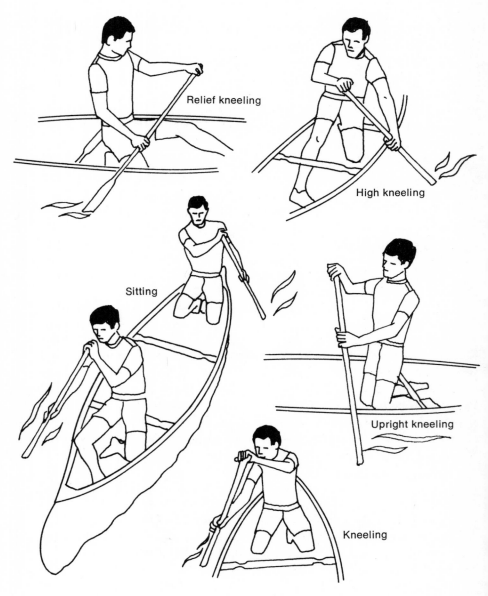

Figure 7.
Paddling positions.

ing on his knees. A variation of the upright kneeling position, the high kneeling position, is used only by racers; in this position the canoeist stretches one leg out in front and positions the lower part of the other, kneeling leg across the bottom of the canoe for stability.

A floor pad is an indispensable piece of equipment for kneeling paddlers. It cushions the knees to protect them from abrasion and soreness.

But kneeling is not the only position from which to paddle. As one marathon racer said, "A lot of good paddling is done sitting down." Though a sitting paddler's weight is higher in the canoe and, therefore, the canoe is more likely to be tipped, the position is not detrimental to good paddling. Sitting canoeists must move more carefully, however, or they will find the position conducive to good swimming as well. It is even acceptable to paddle standing up in a canoe, but the standing position, though good for relief, is not good for novices.

A canoeist must not only determine how he will position himself but where he will sit or kneel in his craft as well. Canoeists paddling alone should be as close to the canoe's center as is reasonably possible. When canoeing in tandem, in a trio, or with cargo, weight should be distributed in a way that will keep the craft in trim—level in the water. The actual positions of canoeists in their craft will vary depending on their weight; lighter persons will have to move farther away from the canoe's center axis to balance the weight of heavier persons, who will position themselves closer to the craft's center.

Though keeping a craft in trim is a basic rule of thumb, occasionally, uneven trim can make for easier stroking and more forward progress in strong winds. A low bow—lowered by shifting weight forward of the canoe's center—offers less resistance when paddling into the wind. And when paddling before the wind, a canoeist can achieve better control of his craft by shifting weight in back of the craft's center to lower the stern. When paddling solo, a paddler can narrow the waterline and thus reduce resistance by tilting his craft slightly to one side.

BASIC PADDLING STROKES

Once correctly positioned, the canoeist is ready to propel his canoe forward, backward, or even sideways. Which strokes the canoeist will choose from his repertoire will depend, however, not only on what maneuver he wishes to execute but also on water conditions and whether or not he is paddling alone or with another person.

Bow Stroke

Most strokes are based on one basic stroke—the bow stroke. To execute this stroke, the paddler grasps the paddle grip with the hand on the side of the canoe opposite the side on which he will be stroking and the shaft with the hand closest to the side on which he will be stroking. There should be slightly more space between the paddler's hands than the width of his shoulders. Holding the blade in a nearly horizontal position, the paddler feathers it ahead over the water and into an upright position. In this position, with his stroke-side arm nearly straight and his other arm nearly bent double, he catches the water with the

Figure 8.
Bow stroke.

blade and then pulls the canoe up to that point by pulling the blade evenly toward him, gradually bending his stroke-side arm and straightening his other arm to do so. To recover and start a new stroke, the paddler allows the paddle to drift back to a position where it can be lifted easily from the water and swung forward again.

The bow stroke is used to move the canoe forward. But suppose the canoeist wants to go backward?

The Backwater Stroke

The reverse of the forward propelling bow stroke is the backward propelling backwater stroke. In fact, even its execution involves an approximate reverse of the bow stroke. With his hands in the same positions as for the bow stroke, the paddler feathers his blade backwards over the water and catches water behind his position in the craft; he then moves backwards through the motions of the bow stroke until the paddle is poised in the "catch" position for the bow stroke. The canoe responds by moving backward through the water. (Canoeists paddling in tandem should curve their strokes in

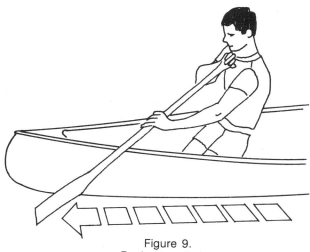

Figure 9.
Backwater stroke.

toward their craft and slightly outward again to make sure the canoe moves backwards in a straight line.)

The Pitch Stroke

To hold a canoe on course, a paddler in the stern can twist or pitch his blade slightly so that water is forced away from the stern. This maneuver is called the pitch stroke.

The J-stroke

Keeping one's craft moving forward in a straight line is frequently a problem. Solo canoeists using the bow stroke on one

Figure 10.
J-stroke.

side of their craft find their canoe turning gracefully away from the direction of their travel. And even paddlers in tandem can have problems if one is stronger than the other. Paddlers can correct their curving course by switching paddling sides frequently or adopting a halting pace, but there is a better solution—the J-stroke. The J-stroke is a modified bow stroke. It follows the same basic motion as the bow stroke until the blade reaches a vertical position near the paddler's body. At that point, with a quick twist of the wrists, the paddler turns the blade outward in a J (or a reverse J) configuration so that water is being pushed away from the boat. This motion corrects the canoe's tendency to curve away from its straight course.

Canoeists can go one step further by feathering the blade at the end of the J-stroke and returning it to the "catch" position underwater. This stroke, which is less tiring once mastered, lessens wind resistance to the canoe's forward motion and slows the canoe. It is called the Canadian stroke.

The Draw Stroke

To move his canoe directly sideways, a canoeist employs the

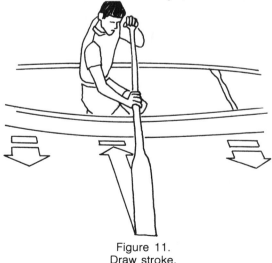

Figure 11.
Draw stroke.

draw stroke. Holding the blade of his paddle parallel to the side of his boat, the paddler reaches out as far as he comfortably can, catches water and draws the canoe toward the paddle, being careful to take the paddle out of the water before it hits the boat. Or the paddler can recover underwater by slipping the paddle sideways through the water to the starting position.

The draw stroke is especially useful in positioning a canoe near a dock. Also, it can be used by paddlers in tandem (stroking on opposite sides of their craft) to execute a quick turn and by the sternman as part of his course-correcting repertoire.

The Pushover and Pry Strokes

The opposite of the draw stroke is the pushover stroke, which also pushes the canoe sideways, but away from the paddler's paddling side. The pushover stroke is another useful steering aid for the sternman in tandem situations. To execute the pushover stroke, the paddler holds the blade parallel to the canoe and dips it into the water close to the side. Then, using his lower arm as a pivot point, he moves the blade sharply outward by drawing his grip hand towards himself. As in the draw

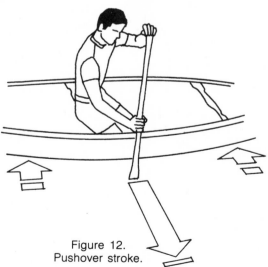

Figure 12.
Pushover stroke.

stroke, the paddle can be recovered through or above the water.

For quicker, more powerful pushover stroke action, the paddle's shaft can actually be rested on the canoe's gunwale for better leverage. This variation is known as the pry stroke. Though it is very effective when the canoeist does not have time to switch his paddle to the other side and execute the draw stroke, it is hard on both paddle and gunwale and should be used only when absolutely necessary—for instance, in white water.

Sweep Strokes

Another set of strokes that should be in every paddler's reper-

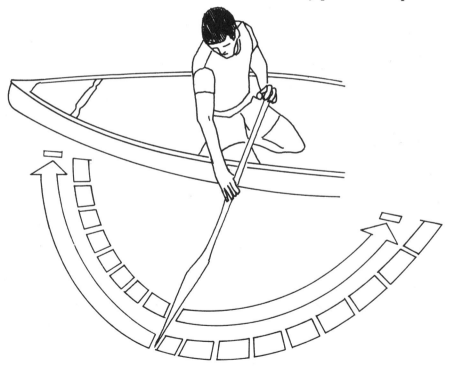

Figure 13.
Sweep and reverse sweep strokes.

toire is the sweep strokes. These variations on the basic bow stroke are the only efficient turning strokes for the solo paddler and can be used in both steering and turning situations in tandem paddling.

The sweep stroke is executed like the bow stroke except that the paddle is positioned just beneath the water's surface and swept horizontally rather than vertically. In the reverse sweep the paddle moves from back to front rather than from front to back.

In essence, sweeps turn a canoe without giving it forward motion. Solo paddlers pivot by executing full sweeps around the center of their canoe. Paddlers working in tandem achieve the same effect with quarter sweeps executed in opposite directions, but in tandem, sweeps are not as effective as draws or prys.

MORE ADVANCED STROKES

The canoeist should complete his repertoire with a few specialized strokes to make white-water navigation easier.

The Sculling Draw

The sculling draw—essentially a figure eight executed with the blade of the paddle at about a 30-degree angle to the canoe—achieves the same effect as the draw stroke, but more efficiently, and, also, it is useful for steadying and slowing a canoe in rapidly flowing water. Solo canoeists use the sculling draw to bring a canoe back into line when it begins to swing by executing the stroke near the swinging end.

Rudder Strokes

In situations in which the craft is moving faster than the current, a canoe's position can be altered merely by holding the paddle at an angle to the water's flow. These positions are known as rudder strokes. The bow rudder, in which the bow paddle is

Figure 14.
Sculling draw.

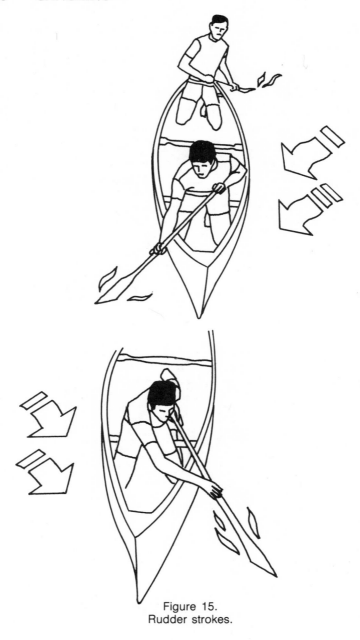

Figure 15.
Rudder strokes.

placed in the water ahead of the canoe at a sharp angle to its bow, will move the canoe toward the paddling side. In a tandem situation, the sternman can increase the momentum of this turn by executing a reverse quarter sweep and leaving his paddle immersed—in the stern rudder position. If the bow paddler positions his paddle in the bow rudder position, but on the side opposite his paddling side, he is doing a cross-bow rudder; the canoe will move toward the paddle and away from the paddler's paddling side.

However, in very swift water, the only safe strokes are the draw and pry. Rudder strokes are recommended for slow-moving water.

Figure 16.
The forward paddler executes the high brace and the aft paddler the low brace; the latter achieves more power to right a tipping boat but at the expense of forward momentum.

Bracing Stroke

A revolutionary new addition to the paddler's repertoire is the bracing stroke, which is executed to avoid an approaching spill or to turn quickly. To do a bracing stroke, the canoeist reaches full out with the paddle and shifts his hips to the side opposite the spill or turn at the same time. The paddle serves as a brake, slowing the craft so that it is either pushed upright or in the direction desired. Braces are either high or low, depending on the angle of paddle in the water. While the technique is useful, it is difficult to master.

GOING UPSTREAM

Not all paddling is done with the current giving an assist. It is sometimes necessary to paddle upstream. In these situations the

Boys jousting in canoes. (Courtesy Sawyer Canoe Company, Oscoda, Michigan)

paddler should use a quick but relaxed recovery to make the most of his energy, seeking out the part of the river where the current offers least resistance (usually near one shore or the other). A canoe poler should adjust the trim of his craft so that the upstream end is higher and escapes the current's pull.

With the above information at his command, the canoeist is prepared for every paddling contingency—and a lot of fun as well.

Courtesy Old Town Canoe Company, Old Town, Maine

6

Toward Safer Paddling

A canoe is as safe or as potentially deadly as a tricycle or a loaded shotgun, depending on the user's training and awareness. This exciting little craft has been much maligned as an unstable, capricous lady, likely to dump her occupants without warning at any given moment. And while it is true that good balance, careful distribution of weight, and judicious ballasting can be factors in keeping a canoe properly afloat, standing, kneeling, moving, and changing position in a canoe can be perfectly safe maneuvers. The secret is in making friends with the canoe—getting to know just how much rocking it will tolerate and precisely what will tip it.

ENTRANCE AND EGRESS

General rules for getting into and out of a canoe include keeping the body weight low, placing one's foot as close to the center line as possible, and gripping a gunwale in each hand. (Gripping each gunwale is a good habit to cultivate under any circumstances. It not only makes entry and exit less traumatic but has a stabilizing effect when movement is necessary while underway.) The paddle can be stowed aboard or placed on the dock beforehand so hands are free for keeping one's balance.

When there are two paddlers to a boat, the sternman enters first and then holds onto the dock while his partner slips aboard; but the sternman exits last, steadying the canoe with a paddle while his paddling mate steps out. Of course, landing conditions vary and will call for adaptations to meet them.

A canoeist's ability to balance safely in a canoe under most conditions he encounters is essential to safe and pleasurable paddling. Though balancing ability grows as familiarity with the craft increases, balance exercises can help. ACA's Gail Cowart, who instructs beginning canoeists in safety, offers this handy exercise for developing a reliable sense of balance: Sit on the side of a dock or at the edge of a pool and bend toward the water slowly until you fall in, feeling for the point at which recovery of an upright position is impossible. Then, repeat the exercise, this time gripping a paddle. As you fall, slap the water hard with the paddle and push yourself back up. With practice, you will be able to push yourself back up to the sitting position even though your head touches the water.

Good canoeists add agility to balancing ability for situations requiring an unexpected exit from a canoe into the water. Though canoeists are more valuable on- than over-board, the unexpected can put the best of them into the drink. There are two rules to remember for these special occasions. One is to avoid capsizing the canoe if at all possible. Chances are that, if the canoe is still afloat, the canoeist can clamber back aboard and resume, though somewhat more damply, his voyage. It is also important to maintain a hold on the canoe. Canoes are very light craft and may go lilting off in a puff of wind faster than the dunked paddler can swim. So the falling canoeist should grab a gunwale as he goes.

Getting back into the tippy canoe can also present problems, but they are not insurmountable. Though specific methods of re-entry depend somewhat on the canoeist, the situation, and the canoe, the basic principle is to avoid overbalancing the

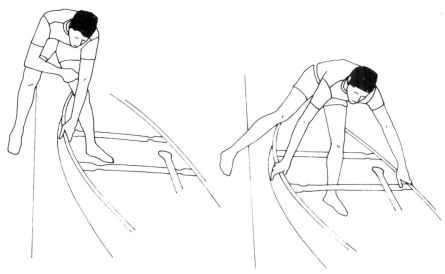

Figure 17.
Entering a canoe from a dock. For debarking simply reverse the procedure.

Figure 18.
Entering a canoe from shore.

This fisherman is familiar enough with his canoe to feel comfortable standing up. However, note that the water is not disturbed by even a ripple. (Courtesy Sportspal, Inc., Emlenton, Pennsylvania)

canoe and capsizing while getting back into the boat. The canoeist prevents capsizing during re-entry by positioning his arms so that when he heaves his weight out of the water onto the canoe it will be distributed nearly equally on both sides of the canoe's center axis. This is best achieved by grasping the gunwale opposite the side of entry with one hand, but the same effect can be attained by grasping a thwart as far toward its opposite side as possible, or even by placing one's hands in the bilge (bottom) of the canoe. Once balanced across the craft, the re-entering paddler squirms and wriggles into a position that allows him to fold, bottom down, into the center of the canoe.

Tandem canoeists overboard have the advantage of being able to balance the canoe for each other by entering from opposite sides one at a time.

CAPSIZING

However graceful a canoeist's unexpected exits and however complete all other precautions, there are times when canoes capsize anyway. The good canoeist prepares for these incidents by capsizing his canoe on purpose to learn as much as he can about how a canoe behaves. What will cause the craft to spill, how it feels to be dumped, what to do when you are dumped, and how well a particular canoe floats are all potential lessons.

The answer to the last question is important. In most instances it is safer to stay with a capsized canoe or kayak than to strike out independently—in search of aid that may not be immediately available through water that may be too cold or fast flowing for safety. Obviously, however, the comforting bulk of a canoe will not be very useful if it sinks.

Canoes made from ABS plastic (Royalex) and those with wood frames float naturally. Other types—such as the ever-popular aluminum models—have flotation added. Most standard commerically made canoes have sufficient flotation material (foamed plastic under the decks at bow and stern and,

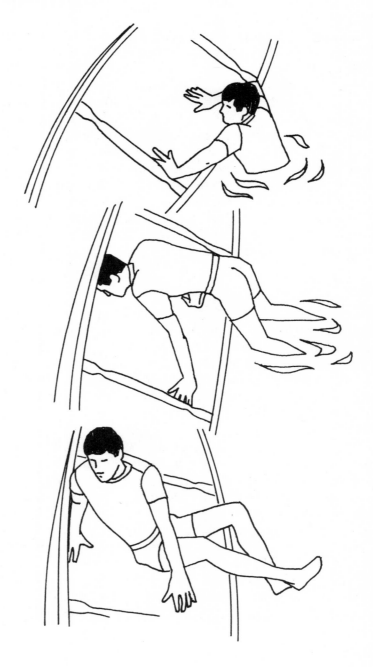

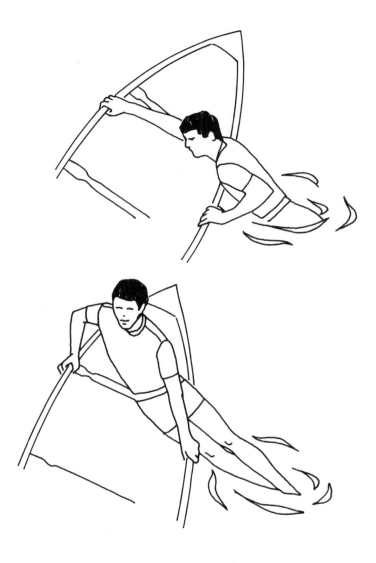

Figure 19.
Two ways to enter a canoe from the water without swamping it.

in some cases, under the seats and gunwales) to keep them afloat when capsized. In fact, in a test of 18 canoe models, all but 1 carried sufficient built-in flotation to support 2 hangers-on, too; and the exception could be easily emptied of water by the "shake-out."

Some models also include built-in air chambers. Black River canoes, for example, have this double flotation, and the manufacturer claims its standard 18-foot canoe will float loaded with water with five adults holding onto the side. Decked canoes and kayaks are usually fitted with styrofoam or air bags that conform to the configuration of the inside of the craft, oc-

Usually it is prudent to stay with your canoe if it capsizes or is swamped. Even when it fills with water, the flotation chambers should keep it afloat and support you in the water until help arrives. These canoeists, however, are close enough to take their canoe to shore themselves. (Courtesy Grumman Boats, Marathon, New York)

cupying most of the below-deck space in the bow and stern.

Once capsized, canoeists in relatively calm water have several alternatives to rescue themselves from their soaking situation. If shore is not too far away, the best course is to paddle in that direction, using the canoe as an aid to buoyancy and resting as often as necessary. On the other hand, if shore is a more distant goal, canoeists should right their capsized craft and climb aboard to paddle home. It is necessary to get in carefully so as not to push the canoe too far underwater, and canoeists should distribute themselves evenly throughout the length of the canoe.

It is also possible, but not easy, to empty the water out of a swamped canoe while it is far from shore. To do this the canoeist, lying very low in the canoe, uses any method possible—usually a vigorous, directed flutter kick—to get enough water out of the canoe so he can sit in his craft without submerging the gunwales. Then, the canoe is laboriously bailed. However, this is not possible to do in high waves.

Very proficient paddlers have a fourth alternative, a maneuver known as the shake-out. This method of emptying a swamped canoe in deep water can enable one lone swamped paddler to be self-sufficient, but it is an arm-deadening drill that requires expert swimming and lots of practice to perfect. It is an advanced technique to be used as a last resort.

The shake-out has two phases. In the first, the paddler positions himself at one end of his canoe and, forcing the near end underwater, thrusts forward and upward. This should empty the canoe of much of the water inside it. The paddler then moves to one side of the canoe where he performs a series of thrusts designed to rid the canoe of the rest of its water. The thrusts must be timed carefully so that when the canoe is thrust away water surges over the gunwale—into the paddler's face but out of the canoe. Maintaining the timing and rhythm of these thrusts requires good swimmer coordination coupled with a powerful frog or scissors kick. When the paddler has freed his craft of water, he climbs back inside according to the method described earlier.

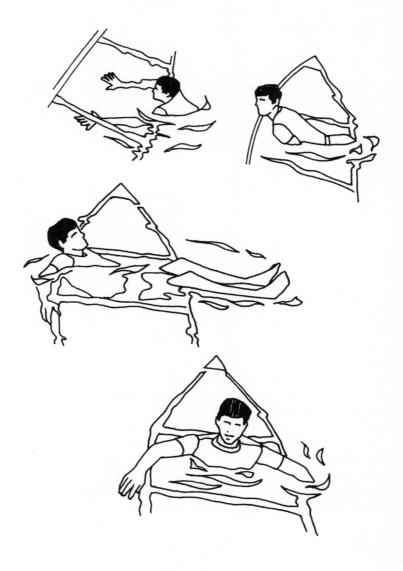

Figure 20.
Boarding a swamped canoe.

Figure 21.
The shake-out.

A canoeist capsizing in white water should try to stay with the canoe, moving to the upstream side of the boat for protection against rocks and other obstacles in the channel. If it does become necessary to abandon the canoe, the canoeist should float downstream feet first, using them (instead of his head) to ward off rocks. If the overboard canoeist swims for it, he must keep his feet high, lest a foot get caught in a fissure in the riverbed, in which case the current could force his head underwater.

OTHER RULES

To insure minimum emergency and maximum paddling, canoeists should follow a few basic rules of the river.

Life Jackets

It is not only folly to venture out without properly approved personal flotation devices but also illegal—an offense punishable by law. And while we have dealt extensively with Coast Guard regulations concerning the required performance of PFDs and the specifics of their selection (Chapter 4), an approved model will not help if it is left at the campsite and may be equally useless if it is tossed carelessly into the canoe's bilge. Yet, despite frequent repetition of the obvious and commonsense admonishment, "Wear them!" scores of lives are lost needlessly each year, because canoeists ignore this basic safety measure—sometimes even when challenging formidable water. In one canoeing mishap reported in the newspaper, a man and his partner, missing and presumed drowned after a spill on the swollen, wind-swept Delaware River, were sitting on their life cushions when the canoe capsized.

Loading

Don't try to put more passengers or gear into a canoe or kayak than it is designed to carry. Check the manufacturer's specifications for recommended capacity and then allow an extra margin of safety. A good rule of thumb is to keep a minimum of four inches of freeboard under favorable conditions and more when conditions are hazardous. Load a canoe so that the center of gravity is close to the center or behind the center of the boat. Also, under cruising conditions, make sure that inboard weight—including that of the canoeist—is distributed close to the keel line of the canoe and as low as possible; this rule will not apply to canoe polers, racers in the high kneeling position, or canoeists in other unusual situations.

Scouting

Never trust a strange river. Study detailed maps of a stream before attempting to paddle it and remember that the

It is obvious that these canoes have been loaded with care. They are level in the water with lots of extra freeboard to accommodate their passengers. (Courtesy Grumman Boats, Marathon, New York)

characteristics of a river can change drastically with the season. The river that is placid and meandering during late summer can be transformed into a raging torrent by the high waters of spring runoff.

Scout rapids or any other dubious stretch in a river—particularly when you're on unfamiliar water—*before* you run it. Certainly, the beginning canoeist shouldn't take the chance of running rapids he hasn't yet developed the skill to handle. The advice of Mark Robinson, a former ranger in Ontario's Algonquin Provincial Park, is worth remembering: "If you come to a rapid and there is a portage around it, take that portage, because the guy who built it probably knew a whole lot more than you do."

Be especially wary of river hazards such as logjams, dams, and other fixed obstacles. Suction near a logjam can drag a canoe or swimmer underwater in a way that leaves little chance for escape, so portage around them whenever possible, particularly in swift water. Dams are always a tricky proposition. Sometimes, at high water, they *look* "runnable" but in fact are not. Should the bow go under and the boat swamp, a powerful, backward-flowing current on the surface can force the canoeist toward the dam and block his escape, a common, serious problem for the inexperienced, incautious canoeist. Avoid entanglement with rocks, low-hanging limbs, fallen trees, and other similar obstacles by moving to the other side of the stream or by portaging. And, if a canoe becomes hung up broadside on a stump, rock, or log, shift weight to the *downstream* side of the canoe and shove off with the paddle. This takes calmness and discipline to accomplish since it is contrary to one's natural reaction to lean away from the obstacle. However, the other course, leaning upstream, can swamp the canoe and cause it to break in half.

Hypothermia

When canoeing in cold water, canoeists and kayakers must be aware of one of the most serious of all boating problems—hypothermia. Hypothermia—a body temperature below normal—occurs quickly in cold water and is accompanied by paralysis. This condition can overtake a capsized paddler almost without warning when he still believes he has enough strength in reserve to reach safety. It is believed that hypothermia may claim more lives than drowning alone. A person dumped into water that is 45°F. may have less than 8 minutes in which to save himself. This fact so governs the thinking of people in the far north that they seldom learn to swim, knowing that it would do them little good. Nor is being physically fit a safeguard. In fact, in this instance, conditioning may be a handicap, since the fit person is likely to have less body fat and therefore less protection.

A last word for newcomers to canoeing: To avoid having their enthusiasm (as well as everything else) dampened, beginners should remember a useful piece of dogma known in paddling circles as Rubin's Rule: Canoeists should not canoe where they wouldn't want to swim. It is counsel the beginning canoeist might well take to heart, as his or her inexperience may very well result in an unexpected dip in the drink. More experienced canoeists must simply take care to avoid situations that exceed their skills or their craft's capabilities.

The start of a race for amateur mixed doubles. (Courtesy Sawyer Canoe Company, Oscoda, Michigan)

7

Getting in Shape
for Canoeing

Inside the church, the midsummer heat was oppressive and the congregation was half asleep. From the pulpit, the minister thoughtfully studied his drowsy flock. Suddenly, he roared, "It's a Goddamned hot day!" At once, his audience was awake and alertly hanging onto every word. "That's what I heard a man say here this morning," he continued, launching into a sermon against blasphemy.

While we have no intention of sermonizing here and the words that follow may not be all that inspirational, we thought we had better recruit the good clergy to help gain your attention. Because we're planning to talk about something that a lot of people don't especially want to hear about (a subject that some view as downright blasphemous)—fitness and exercise. But, without them, one cannot fully appreciate the joys and benefits of canoeing.

As a get-fit and stay-fit sport, canoeing can become an adaptable component of anyone's exercise program. It promotes overall strength and endurance, a supple trunk, well-developed chest, and strong arms and shoulders. Rely on paddling to tighten abdominal muscles and check that tell-tale bulge about the waist. And, although the 17th century French-Canadian voyageur acquired an overdeveloped chest and spindly, atrophied legs, average canoeists don't need to worry about *over-development*. They won't be emulating the voyaguers' 14- to 16-hour, up to 70-mile paddling day.

CANOEING TO FITNESS

Because canoeing is fun, it is a good addition to physical fitness programs that are geared to calisthenics and routine exercises, which often turn out to be shortcuts to boredom. When tedium sets in, motivation collapses and the individual frequently returns to his former, sedentary ways. Canoeing can help keep motivation high.

Remember, though, that while canoeing can help you keep in shape, to get maximum enjoyment from the sport, you must be in condition for *it*. Beginners who lead relatively inactive lives must ease gradually into the sport and slowly build strength and performance. And once in condition, canoeists should paddle regularly—say on weekends and on at least one weekday evening, season permitting—and augment paddling with some supplementary exercise such as regular bicycle riding, or a complementary sport such as tennis or handball to *stay* in good paddling shape!

Because there is an undeniable correlation between exercise and weight control, canoeing also can help an individual stay slim. Those who shrill that exercise merely builds greater appetites and leads to increased food consumption are wrong. The average adult male burns up between 2400 and 4500 calories a day depending upon how much exercise he gets, but active persons may consume up to 6000 calories a day without adding an ounce to their weight. Scientists point out that the addition to one's schedule of only 30 minutes a day of moderate exercise can result in a weight loss of up to 25 pounds per year, assuming food intake remains constant. Relating this to paddling, statistics compiled by the Department of Physiology and

Biophysics of the University of Illinois reveal that a 150-pound person paddling a canoe at 2½ miles per hour will use up 230 calories per hour. And the harder the canoeist strokes, the more calories he will burn off.

A good incentive for regular paddling (although, having explored the joys of canoeing with us, we would hope you won't need urging) is the awards from the President's Council on Physical Fitness. These awards for paddling performance are not for the young, superconditioned, highly trained athlete. Instead, they offer a great second chance to frustrated athletes who never earned a letter at school, but, today, have left the halls of academe far behind. They are designed simply to recognize individuals over 18 years of age who regularly pursue a sport of their choice. (For canoeists, it doesn't matter whether it is flat-water or white-water paddling.) To receive an award in the canoe/kayak division, one must paddle a minimum of 200 miles during a period of 4 months. However, to ensure that participation in one's chosen sport is carried out regularly, no more than 7 miles on any one day may be credited to the total.

A personal log, application form, and other pertinent information are available from Presidential Sports Award, P.O. Box 129, Radio City Station, New York, New York 10019. Upon completion of the required distance, the paddler can send in the log and three dollars—and receive a certificate, pin, and jacket patch. If you rack up enough paddling time in any given four-month period to qualify for the Presidential Award, you probably are well on the way to physical fitness.

STAYING FIT FOR CANOEING

Unfortunately, many canoeists who dedicate much of the summer to getting into reasonable shape spend the winter months getting out of it. For some, the first hint of frost is a signal to turn into an armchair athlete and to become a prime candidate for "loafer's heart," so dubbed because it cannot match a healthy heart in the amount of blood transported with each beat.

One way to beat wintertime sloth is to continue to paddle—indoors. What better opportunity for the beginning canoeist to sharpen his paddling skills and boat-handling techniques and thus heighten his enjoyment of the canoeing season ahead, than to enroll in a course of instruction? To find one in your area, check with local colleges, canoe clubs, YMCAs, and Red Cross chapters. For the intermediate kayaker, a training session in a local swimming pool (again, check the above sources) presents a perfect opportunity to master that elusive Eskimo roll. And for the competitive canoeist and kayaker (and race spectator), there is a growing schedule of indoor slaloms, where a swimming pool serves as the course, with slalom gates suspended above it.

Secondly, there is no reason why one cannot continue supplementary activities during the icebox months. Bicycles can be carried to the basement and set up on rollers; or a stationary exercise cycle can be adjusted to make peddling more difficult as training progresses, and the daily training stint can be accompanied by music, television, or a book. Eminent cardiologist Dr. Irvine H. Page once noted that his exercise cycle provided 20 minutes a day of "unadulterated, uncluttered reading . . . I'm amazed," he said, "at the number of books I'm reading and I'm getting quite a bit of exercise."

Tennis fans will find indoor courts catering to their fast-growing sport. And when fairways freeze over along with canoeing waters, canoeist/golfers might find bowling a worthy substitute—especially in nonleague, "open" play where the action is more sustained. Although not good for developing agility and endurance, bowling helps develop strength in the shoulders, arms, and legs. Since canoeing does little for leg strength, any sports that promote it are an excellent complement to canoeing. Tennis and bicycling also meet this criterion, as do badminton, handball, soccer, and, of course, running.

Many professional athletes condition themselves with running programs. Ohio State football coach Woody Hayes prescribes running as an off-season conditioner, as do many other coaches. However, if you choose this path to winter fitness, keep in mind the maxim of athletic coaches: Train—don't strain. Begin slowly and work up to your top performance over a period of weeks. Most champion distance runners train under a system of interval running: fast running, jogging, then more fast running. Start by running 220 yards; then walk the same distance. Begin with four cycles of this running/walking and gradually increase your effort.

Those intent on getting into shape for racing will do well to follow a program that combines repetition or interval training with weight lifting and such groan-producers as push-ups, pullups, and sit-ups. One successful competitive canoeist even uses translucent surgical tubing hooked to doors and furniture to simulate kayak or canoe paddling strokes.

Courtesy Rivers & Gilman Moulded Products, Inc., Hamden, Maine

8

Planning a Trip

Planning, if not half the fun of a canoe trip, certainly can make the difference between a good or mediocre outing. The David Harrison family, numbering five, had what they describe as the "ultimate wilderness experience" when they paddled 500 miles in two 17-foot canoes to Dawson City on the Pelly and Yukon Rivers in the gold country of the Yukon Territories several summers ago. The Harrisons found that extensive preparations for the trip not only contributed to its success, but also heightened their anticipation. This intricate planning, involving what to take, what to wear, how to pack, and how to arrange transportation to and from the river is not confined, however, to 500-mile odysseys; it is an integral part of just about any canoe trip.

WHERE TO GO

Of course, the first decision is *where* to go. And while the Yukon Territories and other faraway places may have strong appeal, beginning canoeists will be better advised to tackle tried-and-found-navigable waters closer to home. In fact, paddling outings planned before the paddler has invested in his own boat may be dictated by the availability of rental canoes.

Many state tourism or conservation departments maintain lists of canoe liveries and will furnish them upon request. The American Canoe Association (4260 Evans Ave., Denver, Colorado 80222) also can provide information about the location of liveries. Other state agencies, as well, may offer good counsel on where to canoe. For example, the Michigan Department of Natural Resources (Lansing 48926) has produced a fine il- lustrated booklet which describes Michigan rivers that can be canoed with a minimum of danger and a maximum of pleasure, and includes many within easy range of Michigan's big cities but surprisingly "remote." "Minnesota Voyageur Trails" (Minnesota Department of Conservation, Division of Parks and Recreation, 320 Centennial Building, St. Paul, Minnesota 55101, $2.00) provides similarly detailed information on canoe trails, as do many of the free booklets produced by that state. Or start with one of the 10 regional family-oriented canoe trips outlined in the Appendix.

WHAT TO TAKE

What to take on a canoe trip is partly a matter of personal preference. On the other hand, a few basics can go a long way to insuring a smooth and comfortable trip. The list in Chapter 9 was compiled especially for this book by Dave Wainman of Algonquin Outfitters, former chief ranger in Ontario's provin- cial park, who now makes his living renting canoes and outfit- ting clients for canoe/camping trips into the vast wilderness of Algonquin Park. (For tips on packing for children, see Chapter 10.)

Tent and Sleeping Bag

Canoe trip planners should remember that what seems like comfort at home may seem merely heavy after the sixth por-

Kayakers really have to plan ahead, as the capacity of their craft is limited. This trio depends on the larger boat as main provision carrier. (Courtesy Old Town Canoe Company, Old Town, Maine)

tage, and lists of "necessities" should be drawn up accordingly. Weight considerations are especially important in deciding on larger items of equipment such as tent and sleeping bag. If a trip does not involve portaging, a canoe has enough cargo space that a large, heavy tent may be feasible. At the other end of the spectrum, many canoeists eschew a tent altogether, especially if they will be portaging, and stretch out beside their craft beneath the stars instead. Keep in mind, however, that these optimists may end up cramped beneath their craft in the event of rain or mercilessly bitten by insects.

We prefer to compromise on weight and shelter by taking a lightweight tent with nylon taffeta walls that "breathe," a urethane coating on the floor for extra protection against moisture, and a waterproof nylon fly to keep out the rain. And since we like to paddle early and late in the season, we feel that—for us, at least—goose-down sleeping bags are well worth the expense. As well as being lightweight and compressible to fit in a small corner in one's pack, goose down undoubtedly is, ounce for ounce, the warmest filling available. One drawback

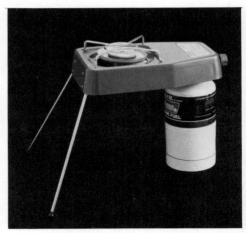

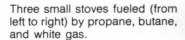

Three small stoves fueled (from left to right) by propane, butane, and white gas.

to goose-down-filled bags is they afford little insulation between sleeper and ground. For this reason, we recommend taking along a foam pad for extra warmth.

Stove

Another piece of equipment of major importance is a stove. Stoves used to be considered a luxury on camping trips, but the new environmental ethic dictates that this heat source supplant the traditional campfire. The latter, as Jerry Sullivan and Glenda Daniel point out in their fine book, *Hiking Trails in the Midwest*, is going the way of the bough bed. "There are so many people using the woods," these authors note, "that fires are just too obtrusive. They use up deadwood that should be rotting back into the soil. They leave ugly black rings, and they carry the risk of setting the whole countryside ablaze."

How large a stove you take depends partially on how many times you portage. A two-burner camp stove is a nice stove to have on a trip without portages. When one does not have to worry about weight, a large-model propane stove of the type marketed by Coleman offers the convenience of a home kitchen. The camp chef can whip up a multicourse gourmet

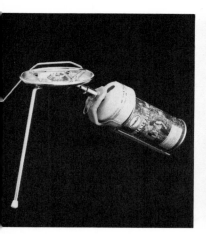 

dinner without muss or fuss. However, to keep the load light, a single-burner model of the type favored by hikers and back-packers is a better choice. And at the lightest end of the weight scale are the tiny white gas stoves—made by Primus, Optimus and Svea—which may weigh less than 20 ounces and fit in the palm of one's hand. These compact stoves work either by self-pressure or a small pressure pump. Butane stoves, which use cartridges as a fuel source, also are lightweight.

Little Luxuries

Little things contribute, also, to the canoe camper's well-being on the water and around the campsite. And, with improvisation a key word in the canoeist's lexicon, the more versatile a product the more valuable.

One not-to-be-left-behind standby is baking soda; it can be used to clean teeth, soothe a stomach, relieve tired feet, smother a small fire or stove flare-up, freshen a coffeepot, scour dishes, and soften socks. (Write to Church & Dwight Company, Inc. [Arm & Hammer], Two Pennsylvania Plaza, New York, N. Y. 10001, for dozens of other suggestions on how to use this inexpensive, multipurpose campsite helper.) Cornstarch is another

Not all luxuries need be versatile. These canoeists have indulged in wine and a bright checked tablecloth.

useful item; invaluable for gravies, it is also effective as a soothing agent on chafed skin. In fact, the list of double-duty items is quite lengthy. Spring-snap clothes pegs can also be used for hanging a tarp to make a shelter. Plastic foam meat trays from the steaks eaten on the first night out will serve as heat-retaining, nonabsorbing plates. Aluminum foil can be used to wrap or package food, to make a reflector oven, or, when crumpled, to clean pots. (Foil is also a good insulator under sleeping bags.) Clear plastic page covers (for ring binders) make fine, waterproof covers for maps when the edges are sealed with transparent tape. Kids' plastic straws double as fire starters; even the tiniest glowing tinder will produce a flame with a straw concentrating a blower's effort. Lemon juice or tomato juice will remove fish odors from the hands of the camp chef. Empty foil packages from dehydrated or concentrated foods, folded in a shirt pocket, make compact, handy drinking cups.

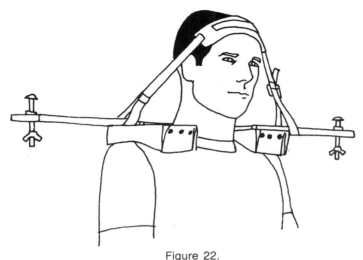

Figure 22.
Tumpline—here attached to a yoke to carry a canoe. However, tumplines can also be rigged to carry gear.

A piece of equipment that can be invaluable on canoe trips
that include a portage is the tumpline. This broad headstrap fits
against the forehead to distribute the weight of the pack more
evenly. The idea is to keep the weight on the spine rather than
the shoulders, at the same time lessening the bite of straps into
soft shoulder tissue. Dave Wainman equips his packs with
tumplines. "With this system," Dave told us, "heavy loads can
be carried without so much as a backache. In fact, many experienced canoeists prefer a tumpline to portage their canoes." Nonetheless, canoeists unused to this head harness may experience
some initial neck discomfort until they get used to it. ("A tortur-
ous invention," one tyro dubbed the tumpline.)

GETTING TO WATER

Once a canoeist has sprung for his own canoe, he must plan for
it, too, and a primary consideration is getting it to water. Unless

the canoe is an inflatable that will pack into a trunk or has its own trailer, which the canoeist doesn't mind towing, it will probably be transported on a cartop carrier.

Carefree car-topping does not happen by chance. On the highway, a car-borne canoe is subjected to powerful stress from all directions, and the boat that is not fastened securely is likely to part company with the carrier along the way. A Texas canoeist, Ken Spencer, learned this the hard way when the two-man spruce and fabric kayak that he had spent many hours building was whipped from the top of his car and damaged. After laboring several nights over repair work, Spencer spent several hours with a slide rule figuring out stresses. He found that at 70 miles per hour (these were pre-energy-crisis days) the backward thrust on the canoe is 68 pounds; that with a crosswind of 30 miles per hour there is a force of 58 pounds pushing against the side of the canoe, too. In simple terms, sloppy tying sends canoes aflying.

We have been supremely confident of car-top canoe security ever since we were given a good lesson in tying by master canoe builder, Elmer Larkin of Sea Nymph. We were transporting a 17-foot aluminum canoe some 150 miles from their Syracuse, Indiana, plant to Chicago. After Larkin's careful strapping and knotting, the 30-mile-per-hour winds howling across the flat midwestern plainsland didn't budge the canoe.

Larkin used four lengths of ¼-inch diameter nylon rope (choosing nylon for its elasticity) and a pair of Grumman aluminum carriers (they are lightweight, use no irksome suction cups, and adjust with an easy-to-turn wheel). The first rope was tied through the towing link in the bow and secured at each end of the front bumper (so that the rope formed an inverted V). A second length of rope was used in the same way at the stern, and affixed to the rear bumper. The third length of rope was brought over the hull and secured to the front carrier at each side, close to the canoe's gunwales, to prevent sideways slippage. The fourth piece of rope was used to repeat this procedure with the rear carrier.

CONSUMER GUIDE TO CARTOP CARRIERS

Grumman Boats, Marathon, New York 13803

Kari-Lite, Crawford Industries, P.O. Box 31, Marshall, Michigan 49068

Lincoln Fiberglass, Inc., Route 62, Stow, Massachusetts 01775

Old Town Canoe Company, Old Town, Maine 04468

Rubber Rope and Packaging Company, Inc., 412 See Gwun Avenue, Department 150, Mount Prospect, Illinois 60056

Sportspal, Inc., Drawer T, Emlenton, Pennsylvania 16373

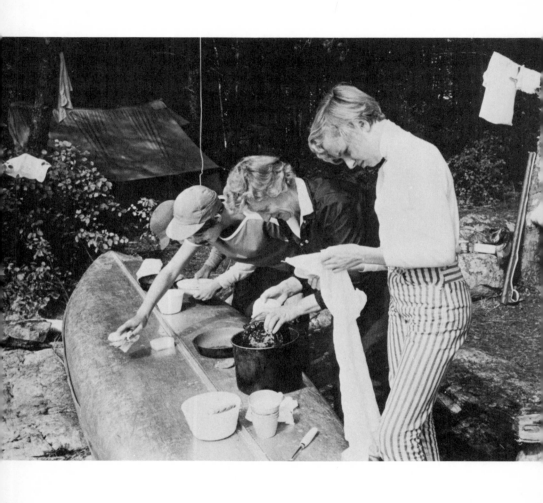

9

Camping by Canoe

Paddling purists, as we've said, paddle for paddling's sake. They delight in the science of the strokes they execute so effortlessly; they enjoy competing against each other, distance, the clock, and, often, the water itself. But, for another host of canoeists—fishermen, bird watchers, naturalists, outdoor chefs, and the like—the canoe, while enjoyable, is essentially a vehicle to transport them to their guiding pleasures. And we confess that the secondary pleasures of canoeing are infinitely appealing, on occasion, to us as well. To drift and dream on a summery afternoon, caring naught for the symmetry of strokesmanship; to paddle before the sun is yet warm in the morning to pick breakfast berries on a distant shore; to search for trout in a tranquil pool in evening; or to find and organize a snug campsite in the golden light of sunset—life is made of these canoeing pleasures, too. In this chapter we offer a few tips to make the most of canoeing's bonus benefits.

PORTAGING

The first problem with fishing, photographing, or camping by canoe is getting to an appropriately remote spot. Some inviting destinations may necessitate a portage—or two or ten.

Though a nuisance, portaging is bearable if approached in a sensible manner. If you know ahead of time that you will be making portages, you have undoubtedly planned to pack as lightly as possible in portable containers such as packs or duffle bags, and you have remembered to bring your tumpline.

However, there remains the paramount problem of the canoe, which, however graceful in the water, behaves exactly like a beached seal when removed from this liquid medium. Though two canoeists can carry their craft for short distances by grasping opposite gunwales and balancing the canoe between them, the best method over longer portages is for two people to carry the canoe upside down on their shoulders.

The first step after the canoe has been taken out of the water is to attach the carrying yoke. If one man will be carrying the craft the yoke should be slightly in front of the canoe's center axis, since it is easier to pull the front of the canoe down than to

A one-man canoe carry with the yoke attached slightly in front of the center axis. For portages of any distance, however, the two-man carry is better. (Courtesy Core-Craft, Bemidji, Minnesota)

Figure 23.
The two-man carry.

push it up. (A properly "yoked" canoe can be balanced with one hand.) If the yoke is a makeshift one of paddles lashed to thwarts (see Chapter 4), use sweaters or other rolled clothing to cushion its weight on your shoulders. Carrying yokes rigged with a tumpline so that one's head and shoulders can bear some part of the burden further ease the strain of portaging.

With the yoke in place, the next step is to hoist the craft into position. Although two city bumpkins of our acquaintance, who embarked on a northwoods canoe/camping trek without knowledge of the proper hoisting technique, spent considerable time along the trail looking for forked trees to prop up their canoe while one of them slipped underneath, there is an easier lifting method (see Figure 24).

Turn the canoe, with carrying yoke installed, on its side, keel toward you, and reach for the center. Grasp the yoke. Then crouch with knees bent, lift the canoe, and slide it onto your lap (it should be in floating position, seats upward). Grasp the far side of the yoke with your left hand and lift and roll the canoe over, easing the yoke onto your shoulders.

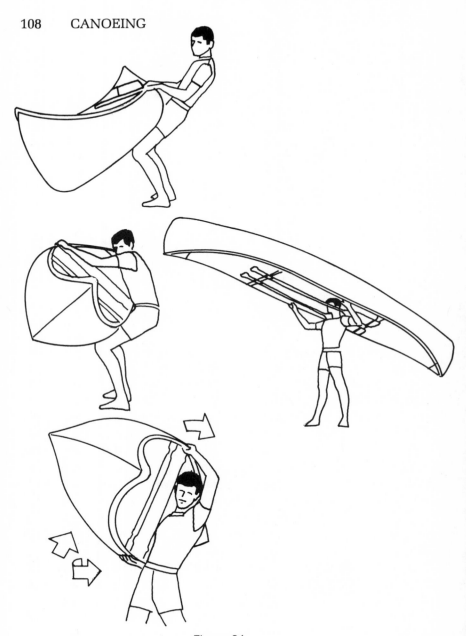

Figure 24.
Lifting the canoe into carrying position.

Sometimes the terrain along the riverbank adjacent to an obstacle or a very wild rapids makes portaging impossible. The woods may be too thick or the drop of shore too steep for safe carrying. One solution to this problem is to "line" or "track" the canoe through the unnavigable spot. To execute this maneuver, ropes between 50 and 100 feet in length are tied both to bow and stern. With a paddler controlling each rope, the craft is guided through the impassable section.

Figure 25.
Tracking a canoe.

CAMPSITES

Another important aspect of comfort to consider on a trip of any length is where to stop for the night. Nothing can ruin a good trip faster than a bad night's sleep, not unusual in the average forest, which dispenses to the unwary such delights as insects and swamps.

The best way to avoid uninvited guests and uncomfortable camping conditions is to select every campsite carefully. This means starting the search soon enough in the afternoon so that dusk does not catch you unsettled. Look for a site that offers some shelter from wind and rain (though enough wind to keep the flies away is nice), that is high enough for good drainage in case of showers, and far enough away from swampy places to avoid mosquitoes. A good view from the open tent flap is a bonus. And know your river; some rise unexpectedly from reservoir releases.

Water is another necessity. Though pure water, which can be dipped for use directly from a stream or spring, is still available in isolated areas, water pollution is increasingly a problem. If there is any question, boil the water or use halazone tablets or iodine in the ratio of 10 drops to a gallon to purify it before you use it.

Also, be sure that camping is allowed at the spot you choose. If the land is private, you need to get permission before you camp.

MEALS

Once settled securely for the night, the canoeing crew is bound to be hungry. Since canoeists will want to travel as light as possible on an extended canoe trip, cooking utensils and food supplies should be kept to a minimum. (And check stream regulations on trash disposal, fires, etc.) However, with nested saucepans, a skillet, and a coffeepot, the canoeside chef has the basic implements to conjure up some ambrosial camp meals.

Two tired young canoeists settle down to eat.

And planning one-dish meals—a necessity with the limitations of one or two stove burners—insures that everything is ready at once; cleanup is easier, too. Stews and hearty soups provide nourishing and tasty one-pot meals and take advantage of whatever ingredients are available. Similarly, many one-skillet omelet dinners can be created from fresh or powdered eggs and the addition of a variety of meat and vegetable (canned or packaged) combinations.

Using leftovers is another food-conserving knack that can be applied around the campsite, as well as in the home kitchen. When the fishing is good, there is a tendency to waste leftovers.

Instead, store remaining cooked fish in a plastic bag and combine it with canned soup to make a hearty chowder. Honey makes an unlikely but eminently compatible accompaniment. And just as chowder originated as a community dish, when village fishermen in France contributed part of their catch to the communal stewpot, so canoeists can make chowder the excuse for a campsite get-together, with each participating canoeing family contributing some fish.

The following recipe comes courtesy of Coleman Company's Thayne Smith, a veteran outdoor writer, and Pillsbury Publications. Together they offer Easy Fish Chowder complemented by squares of hot cornbread and honey as a good supper for a cool evening.

Easy Fish Chowder:
   1 pound fish, cooked and cubed (about 2 cups)
   2 cans (10½ ounces each) condensed cream of potato soup
   1 soup can of milk (about 1 cup)
   4 to 6 slices crisp bacon, crumbled
   1 can (1 pound) sliced carrots, drained
   2 tablespoons instant minced onion or ½ cup chopped onion
Combine all ingredients in a large saucepan. Heat through. Makes six to eight servings.

While we like to do as much of our campsite cooking as possible from scratch, we do acknowledge that we are bucking the trend and even admit that taking advantage of the many available convenience foods makes good sense. Canned or freeze-dried meats, instant potatoes, packaged sauce and gravy mixes, and instant desserts are all compact, lightweight, and need no refrigeration. They make meal preparation speedy and simple. In fact, many products can be prepared right in the package—just add water and stir; no dishes to clean. However, since many of these meals-in-a-package leave much to be desired in terms of taste, campsite cooking ingenuity with food should not be abandoned altogether. In these days of freeze-dried ice cream, we tend to think kindly of an innovative friend, outdoor writer Patrick Snook, who, on the occasion of his daughter's birthday during a bush trek, used his homemade reflector oven to bake a layered birthday cake.

CHECKLIST—PACKING FOR A CANOE TRIP

Camping Equipment

Packs—with or without tumplines
Tents
Cook kit
Plates
Cups
Eating utensils—forks, spoons
Bowls
Bread knife
Serving spoon
Potholder
Can opener
Spreading knife
Mixing jug
Plastic food and egg containers
Food and equipment bags
Two towels
Map wallet with maps
Salt and pepper shakers
Pot cleaners
Matches in waterproof container
Toilet paper

Sleeping bags with liners
Sleeping pads or air mattresses
Soap—hand and laundry
Ax
Saw
Grate
Reflector oven
Folding shovel
Ponchos
Tarps
Personal flotation devices
First aid kit
2 compasses (a spare is important)
Stove and fuel
Flashlight
Water purification tablets
Canoe repair kit (boat type)
Carrying yoke (if there will be portages)
Water container of some kind
Candles
Long rope (50 feet)

Personal Equipment

Two good rugged outfits of clothing, two pairs of socks, two sets of underwear, one pair of heavy boots, one pair of soft shoes, toilet articles, towel, raingear, cap or hat are necessities. Such items as camera, fishing equipment, bathing suit, flashlight, pajamas, etc., are optional, depending upon personal needs and the nature of the trip. In many areas of the northland, long underwear and extra jackets or sweaters are advisable during the early and latter parts of the season. Remember to keep personal articles to a minimum, especially if you are planning portages.

Provisions

Following is a typical weekend menu recommended by veteran canoeist, home economist, and outdoorswoman Harriett Barker, from her book, *The One Burner Gourmet**

Saturday breakfast: Canned juice
Granola and milk (Mix dry milk and coffee lightener, half and half into the dry granola. Add *hot* water for a delicious hot cereal.)
Poached eggs or soft-boiled eggs, cooked in the coffee water
English muffins, split, buttered, and toasted in the frying pan
Coffee or hot chocolate

Saturday dinner: Hot bouillon
Beans
Green salad, washed and trimmed at home and put in a plastic bag
Rolls heated over the pot of beans on an inverted lid or foil pan, covered
Instant pudding and cookies
Hot tea

Sunday breakfast: Juice crystals mixed with warm water
Bacon

---

*©Harriett Barker 1974, *The One Burner Gourmet*, Greatlakes Living Press, P.O. Box 11311, Chicago, Illinois 60611. Reprinted by permission.

Pancakes and honey or marmalade
One fried egg apiece
Coffee or hot chocolate
Lunches: Drink mix with sugar added (include plastic container
and cups)
Honey spread
Peanut butter
Cheese spread
Dry salami (include sharp knife and a cutting board)
Crackers
Cinnamon graham crackers
Dried fruits (raisins, prunes, apples)
Fresh fruit, (apples, oranges)
Toasted sunflower seeds for cracker spreads
Fruit logs for mid-meal snacks
Plastic bags for mid-meal snacks
Several plastic spreading knives, paper towels, table-
cloth

For lunch on a cold day, hot instant bouillon, or the individual cups of soup are easily heated in Sierra metal cups on your one-burner stove.

10

Canoeing with the Kids

Call off the babysitter or your mother-in-law. Unless you are planning to spend the weekend challenging wild water, there really is no reason to have qualms about taking children with you on that canoe cruise and campout. All it takes to make a river trip safe and enjoyable for adult and youngster alike is some thoughtful planning, a positive attitude, a dash of imagination, and adherence to a few commonsense rules. For, while there is nothing to match sharing with children the joy of discovering nature, a poorly planned trip can be disaster. As one mother lamented after a calamitous weekend afloat with two very young children: "Believe me, there are few things worse than being penned up at close quarters with a couple of cranky kids." Admittedly, she was distraught and probably exaggerating, but the experience was enough to make her vow not to take the children into a canoe again until they were well into grade school.

Yet it need not be that way. We have canoed with our children, without trauma, since both were quite young. In fact, David had barely graduated from kindergarten when we made

117

our first family canoe/camping trip into the wilderness of Ontario's Algonquin Provincial Park. He had learned to swim (after a fashion), and we fitted him with a life jacket that allowed freedom of movement. The three portages we made added welcome variety to long stretches of boat travel across the preserve's large lakes. We were careful, though, to choose a route with short, easy portages, avoiding the rugged two-milers we had made on earlier, childless occasions. On long hauls, young children quickly burn themselves out, because they lack the experience to pace themselves to conserve strength. As it was, David and Glynis enjoyed helping out both on the short portages and with campsite chores.

Diversion is probably the key to canoeing contentment for young paddlers. Schedule frequent stops for play and rest. Let a preschooler take along his rubber duck or favorite float toy to troll on a string. Or, better still, outfit him with a miniature paddle so he can help propel the boat.

With a working knowledge of riverside wildlife and vegetation, parents can turn a family canoe trip into a fascinating and lasting lesson in natural science. Exploring a nature trail, for example, can be a memorable family adventure. Let the youngsters collect leaf specimens and hunt for nature's bounty—blueberries and chokecherries, asparagus and pungent wild onions. Help them discover how the shredded leaves of tender young dandelions can add zest to scrambled eggs or how wild strawberries that have grown in open areas seem to be sweeter than those grown in the shade. Tell them how the scent of skunks causes temporary blindness when it hits animals in the face, and how, conversely, leaves of sage provide a natural deodorizer.

There is a whole new world awaiting those who dare to view the outdoors through the eyes of a child. Children can provide the impetus for parents to look more carefully at their surroundings. Help a child count the number of colors reflected in a river and the number of shades of green in the summer woodland. Examine with a child that model of industry, the anthill, and the skillful craftsmanship that goes into the intricately woven nest of a riverside warbler.

June Morgan, who writes a column for *Canoe News*, the quarterly publication of the United States Canoe Association, tells of taking five-year-old twins on a 30-day, 300-mile canoe trip into the Canadian wilderness. The children slept as the adults paddled and were ready, when the time came to set up camps, to explore the surrounding area. One treasured photograph is of the discovery of the dark brown egg of a loon.

We made one memorable family canoe trip with friends who recently had moved to the Midwest from California. Jack Coughlan had some previous paddling experience, but Pat and the two girls, ages 10 and 12, never had canoed before. For the initiation to the time-honored practice of traveling in an open canoe, we chose the Pigeon River in northeastern Indiana, a gentle flowing, tree-canopied river. Its mild disposition and scenic banks were perfect for turning beginners into converts. (Unfortunately, too many neophyte paddlers attempt to run white water beyond their meager skills and become permanently put off by some harrowing experience—if, indeed, that is the worst fate to befall them.)

For the Pigeon trip, our friends rented a 15-foot Browning AeroCraft aluminum canoe, which they found easy to maneuver and rugged enough to take the punishment of sliding over the logs that occasionally jam stretches of the Pigeon. Dick Cagley, the livery owner, shuttled us to our point of departure near the town of Howe, made sure the youngsters had their life jackets on securely, and offered a short primer in basic paddling strokes and safe onboard conduct. It wasn't long before Pat and the kids were calling the paddle a paddle, not an "oar," and busily attempting to identify the scenery sliding past—sycamores, oaks, hickories, cottonwoods, aspen, and a large stand of tamarack.

The five-mile, four-hour trip provided a good demonstration of what a canoe trip can mean to children. We saw a blue heron wading near the bank and a muskrat, which dove as we approached. When we stopped to rest, a pair of reluctant salamanders was held in captivity long enough to stage a race. The children also collected empty shells of freshwater clams strewn on the stream's shallow bed. The adults also had their day when we stopped by a grassy knoll to picnic on sandwiches and fruit we had packed. The kids romped and we stretched out to savor the serenity of the riverside scene.

This leisurely cruise was long enough to give tyro canoeists a variety of experiences but short enough that the children did not get bored. Certainly, city-bred offspring should be introduced gradually to life in the wild, and two-hour or half-day canoeing trips are an ideal way.

SPECIAL ADVICE

Camping out with Mother Nature can be a good experience. On the other hand, when nature is unknown, it can have a frightening effect on children. To make their vacation—and therefore yours—enjoyable, follow the tips below.

Packing

Take along enough dry clothes for an emergency, but don't try to pack everything a child owns. One experienced canoeing family allows for each child one change of clothes, a swimsuit, and a lightweight jacket for one week of canoeing. They meet additional needs by washing what they have brought. Hooded sweatshirts are ideal in cooler paddling weather.

Pack children's clothing near the top of the duffel or pack so that it is quickly available. And, for the very young, pack especially carefully, being sure to include such necessities as talc, romper outfits, and dry diapers. Richard Langer, author of *The Joy of Camping*, a fine book about self-propulsion in the wilderness, took his daughter along while she was at a very tender age and observes that the paper diapers that so many mothers find convenient are disposable only for as long as one

Setting up camp early and serving food quickly help children enjoy canoe trips.

stays close to civilization. The Langers used cloth diapers for their infant daughter, washed them as necessary, and left them out as they traveled; the sun then dried and sterilized them.

Acclimatization

Before embarking on a trip, let a youngster get the feel of the boat on a local pond or in the swimming pool. You should not suddenly spring a life jacket on a child. Get one that fits comfortably, without constricting the child (see Chapter 4 for tips on selection) and let the youngster get used to it by wearing it around the house for a while. National Marathon Canoe Champion Roland Muhlen went even further when he built a 54-inch cedar strip canoe-shaped crib for his infant. At two months, the baby probably had accumulated more canoe hours than many paddlers put in during a lifetime.

Snacks

As many mothers readily will testify, some youngsters aren't quiet unless they are sleeping or eating (some would add "fighting"). So keep snack foods handy when paddling. Dry cereal, raisins, fruit, and hard candy are good for quick energy. Or combine various ingredients into "gorp." Though there seem to be almost as many recipes for this food as there are canoeists in need of pep, one popular combination blends raisins, peanuts and chocolate-covered candies (the kind that melt in the mouth rather than in the hand). Pretzels, perennial favorites of the munching set, and beef sticks make good hot-weather treats, because they help replace salt lost through perspiration.

Flexibility

Remember that your children are on vacation, too, and allow them to deviate from their normal schedules to take advantage of what their unusual surroundings have to offer. If you are camped at a site where campfires are permitted, let your child stay up a little later to enjoy the experience and roast a marshmallow or two. And be prepared to tolerate the extra grubbiness that is an inevitable adjunct of youngsters experiencing the freedom of the outdoors as they explore each new campsite. But, of course, police the area for such hazards as poison ivy.

Education

Don't encourage children to pick wildflowers or strip bark off trees; a canoe trip is a good time for a youngster to learn to *appreciate* natural beauty. Investment in an inexpensive camera may yield handsome dividends in happy moments during the trip and photographic memories afterwards. Youngsters can also engage in such sound diversions as making casts of animal tracks, compiling a nature notebook, creating rubbings from historic markers and milestones you find along the way, and collecting driftwood and other found objects to make jewelry, furniture and art constructions.

You are certain to find that, if sensibly planned, a canoeing trip with children is rewarding for everyone concerned.

Courtesy Grumman Boats, Marathon, New York.

II

Reading Rivers and Rapids

Regardless of how safe your equipment, how careful your planning and packing, how balanced your loading, canoeists who can't read a river aren't home free. Not only must paddlers know the hydraulics of the channel, they must be aware of what to watch for on the banks of the stream as well.

MAPS

The first lesson is to learn as much as possible before even launching a canoe on the stream you plan to paddle. There is much to be learned, for instance, from a good topographic map (or"topo"). It shows changes in elevation, which in turn show when to expect fast water. For example, lines on the map that are close together indicate a steep hillside and thus the probability of deep water in narrow channels bordered by cliffs or other inhospitable countryside. On the other hand, lines farther apart signal gently sloping terrain, potentially good spots to set up camp at night. Topo maps also show swampy and shallow spots and the location of such landmarks as trails, buildings, mines, railroads, power lines and other features that might serve as navigational aids.

Topo maps are a good way, too, to assess a river's gradient, one important indication of how fast the water will be flowing in the channel. The maximum gradient that canoes can navigate is 60 feet per mile, but be aware that this is tough canoeing. Beginners should choose a much gentler slope to sharpen up their paddling skills.

Use a topo to get a true compass reading. Virtually all maps are drawn to true north, or the North Pole. However, compasses usually point to magnetic north which is near, but not at, the North Pole. Topo maps show magnetic variation in the margin, which will help you compute the reading for true north.

Also, when studying your topo, look for the places where streams join the river you will be paddling. The meeting of main stream and tributary can result in rapids, spilled-out boulders, fresh water, or a delta suitable for a campsite and good fishing.

Many outdoors shops carry topographic maps, or you may purchase them directly from the U.S. Geological Survey, which has offices in Washington, D.C. (for maps east of the Mississippi) and in Denver, Colo. (for maps west of the Mississippi). Those wishing to paddle in Canada may wish to obtain maps in the National Topographic series from the Map Distribution Office, Department of Mines and Technical Surveys, 615 Booth Street, Ottawa, Ontario, Canada.

Another prepaddling reference is the Randy Carter River Marking system, which rates the height of a river with measurements that start at zero—which equals the minimum canoe-navigable height of three inches—and expresses depth beyond three inches in increments of one foot, up to the maximum "safe" level of five feet. (Carter's 195-page book on the subject may be obtained from the author, 158 Winchester St., Warrenton, Virginia 22186.) These gradings are marked by yellow paint at various locations along many rivers. And, through an informal arrangement, canoeists may telephone ahead to designated reporting stations to find the river level at any given time.

With prepaddling homework complete, you're ready to go, but don't rely exclusively on the maps you've studied. Not only do characteristics of rivers change somewhat from season to season due to floods and erosion, but maps are not foolproof in the first place. They are meant as an aid, not the final word.

Another indicator of what is going to happen ahead is the river bank. Michael learned this early in his white-water paddling days when he went canoeing with an old-timer. At one point, Mike's wise companion pointed out that the tree line was sloping down more rapidly and the channel was narrowing, forecasting fast-moving water ahead. Sure enough, there were rapids around the next bend. So watch the river for any telltale signs of what's to come.

SCOUTING

Once you've ascertained that rapids are your lot, pull over to shore and look them over before you "chute" on through. Although sometimes the prudent paddler will simply discover what combination of hasty delights the channel has in store, on other occasions the river will present a choice of several routes.

The appearance of these alternatives may be deceiving. The route that seems smoothest might be the most violent, because its descent begins later than the others and is therefore more rapid and steeper. Conversely, the passage which begins to show turbulence earliest has a longer and gentler gradient and will provide the most comfortable ride. This is the "chicken" chute, so called because it is favored by beginners and cowards. Expert paddlers with decked boats usually prefer the challenge of the more difficult course through the turbulent water. Also, scouting canoeists can locate the eddies, less turbulent spots where a tired paddler can stop to rest.

RAPIDS

Paddlers who add to this prudent preparation for rapids running some knowledge of river hydraulics—the factors shaping water flow—will be sitting pretty. To read a river properly, it helps to gauge its discharge (water volume), gradient and resulting velocity, and to know the reasons and effects of eddies, backrollers, souse holes and other characteristics of flowing water. Only then can the canoeist be sure of working with the current rather than against it.

Velocity

Velocity is one of several measurements of a stream's navigability. The greater the volume of water, the narrower the channel, and the steeper the gradient, the greater will be the velocity.

Physical Hazards

However, barring an unexpected spill over a waterfall—why did you think scouting was important?—the volume, channel depth, gradient, and velocity do not, in themselves, make rapids hazardous for the average paddler. Rather, it is the interaction of these characteristics with the physical hazards that causes excitement—steep drops, violent crosscurrents, whirlpools, tall irregular waves, and/or a lengthy series of connecting rapids.

When it comes to negotiating rapids, "V" is an important letter. When riffling on the surface of the water forms a "V" *with the point downstream*, it signifies an upstream opening created by water flowing between two obstructions, which means a safe passage—Victory. On the other hand, when the point of the "V" is upstream, it means that the obstruction is directly in your path—a hazard that could Vanquish you.

Chutes. The victorious passage is called a chute or sluice—any fast-flowing channel. It can be located between boulders or converging banks or anywhere else a high volume of water is forced through a narrow space. Look for an exhilarating ride, or, if you are a timorous paddler, look for the quieter waters of the aforementioned "chicken" chute, although this latter is not always available.

Learning which chute to shoot is part of learning to read a river. (Courtesy Core-Craft, Bemidji, Minnesota)

A veteran canoeist once told us that there were two ways of shooting a chute: "Either you can run faster than the current and let sheer speed carry you through or you can paddle slower than the current and use paddling technique to maneuver your way through." Both require skill, because the obstacles remain the same. But the former method necessitates split-second timing and controlled paddling power while the latter requires agility and a large repertoire of strokes. Another important factor to consider in evaluating a chute is the size of the waves below it. They are called standing waves or haystacks.

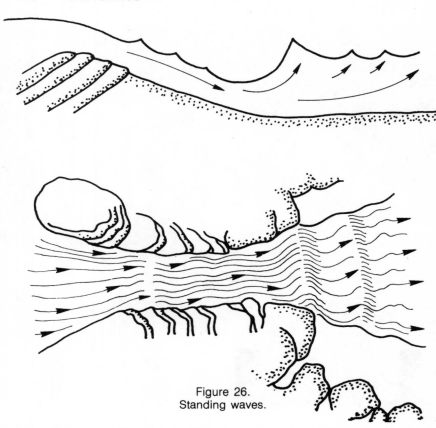

Figure 26.
Standing waves.

Standing Waves. When water rushes down a chute, it is slowed so quickly by slower flowing water at the bottom that it backs up into standing waves or haystacks, which signify the deepest part of the channel. If these waves are more than a foot high, you're likely to swamp unless you use a spray deck and are endowed with more than a modicum of canoeing skills. Novice and intermediate paddlers should look for an easier passage.

Beware also of hidden boulders or other obstructions amid the standing waves. They will be noticeable because they interrupt the wave pattern, causing it to be irregular.

Ordinarily, when entering the waves, the paddler should either slow his craft so that the canoe will ride on or near the

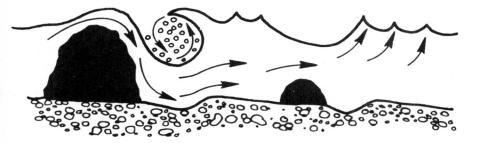

Figure 27.
Souse hole and back waves.

waves' crests or angle the canoe upon entering them to give the bow lift. The amount of water shipped depends on the design of the canoe and how it is loaded in addition to the canoeist's skill.

Back Waves and Souse Holes. When water falls steeply over a gradient and curls back, it creates a back wave or backroller. Given the right combination of conditions, this backroller will join with an eddy into a souse hole. When canoeists see a depression in a rapids with water falling into it from all directions, they are looking at a souse hole. Souse holes are for experts and experts only, and even then they should be entered with forethought and a prayer.

Eddies. When the experienced canoeist tires of battling his way

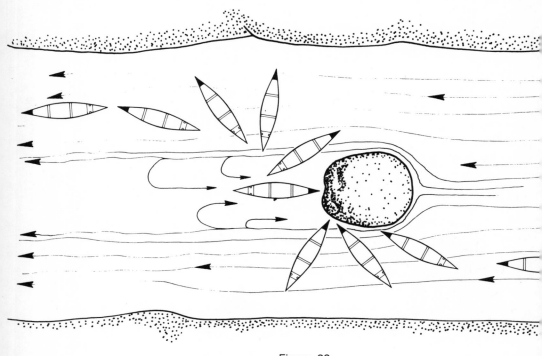

Figure 28.
A canoe enters an eddy to rest a moment and then exits to continue downstream.
Notice how the bow is pointed upstream when exiting to prevent the canoe from
spinning.

through chutes, over (hopefully) standing waves and around souse holes, he looks for an eddy to rest in. An eddy is a gentle upstream swirl of current that occurs on the downstream side of an obstruction, usually a rock or boulder, as a result of water closing the gap behind the obstruction as the main current flows past. The current in an eddy is relatively calm and tends to flow in a circular course. As a rule of thumb, the length of an eddy is double the width of the obstruction that causes it. Size is the only major varying characteristic of eddies. Because eddies are calm, they are resting places and may be useful stepping stones in crossing turbulent water.

However, though eddies, themselves, pose no danger to the

canoeist, the current flowing past the obstruction to create the eddy, can get the paddler into trouble. Entering and exiting eddies, therefore, require good timing and expert maneuvering. It is possible to enter an eddy by paddling hard toward the eddy in a line almost at the obstruction so that the current has no opportunity to catch the stern and spin the canoe downstream. Once inside the quiet water, the craft must be quickly halted with backwater strokes.

Or the paddler can draw his craft lengthwise alongside the eddy and enter it stern first by using a hanging draw stroke. Once locked into an eddy, a canoe will stay there almost indefinitely because there is little motion in the water.

To leave the eddy, the paddler edges the bow upstream so the current will catch it. As the canoe turns downstream with the current, he leans into a brace stroke toward the downstream side to prevent swamping.

To move from shore to shore without being swept inconveniently downstream, a canoeist can use eddies as stepping stones to "ferry" his way across. After plotting a path from eddy to eddy across the current, the canoeist noses out into the fast-moving water with his bow pointed upstream and paddles hard, keeping his canoe at an upstream angle across the current until he reaches the next eddy. He repeats the process until he has crossed the river.

Types of Rapids

Not all rapids offer the terrifying variety of hazards described above, and to help canoeists, the rapids to many rivers have been subjected to classification. Rivers classified as Grade I and II are generally suitable for beginners. Though these rivers may have large volume, they flow in broad channels down gentle gradients. These waters are relatively easy to paddle, obstructions can be easily seen, waves that occur are small, and when passages are narrow they are generally clear, with a minimum of spray.

It is on rivers such as these that the learning canoeist can en-

In some rapids, such as this one, waves are small and obstructions are easily seen. (Courtesy Old Town Canoe Company, Old Town, Maine)

counter riffles. Riffles, which are very gentle rapids, are characterized by tiny waves, an obstruction-free channel, and shallow water. They are the ideal place for novices to gain confidence in their canoe-handling techniques. Riffles do not behave in the exact same manner as bigger rapids, because they are not so powerful. Also, they may be so shallow that paddles become virtually useless except as rudders. But riffles are similar enough to rapids to give the novice a preview of the excitement to come.

Since the river over riffles is normally quite shallow, the canoe may scrape bottom, but don't worry about it. As Ralph Frese, Illinois's "Mr. Canoe," once said: "You can be proud of the scratches on the bottom of your canoe, because they are from honest use. But be ashamed of the scratches on the sides as they are signs of abuse."

On the other side of the rapids coin are waters classified Grades III-V. These require experience, skill, a canoe equipped with cover, good teamwork when traveling in tandem, and, *most emphatically*, a Type I PFD. A crash helmet may also be a good idea. Though no two rivers are alike and there is no formula for mapping a course through a particular rapids, adherence to two overriding principles will make an uneventful passage through rough water more likely. First, keep your boat aligned with the central current; and, second, when, for some reason, whether planned or otherwise, the canoe is broadside to the current, *lean downstream* to avoid swamping the canoe.

No two rivers are the same, and, worse yet, the perplexed paddler cannot even count on one river being the same all the time. They are too much at the mercy of the seasons and the elements. A flash flood can change the physical makeup of a river overnight, gouging out new holes in the shoreline and new bends and twists in the old bed. This is to say nothing of the new boulders, felled trees, and other debris caught up by the flood that are deposited randomly along the way as the water slows. But perhaps that is part of the charm of the paddler's art. Even the most cunning canoeist can never be quite sure of what is around the next bend.

Running many rapids requires experience, skill, and good teamwork when traveling in tandem. (Courtesy Sawyer Canoe Company, Oscoda, Michigan)

Courtesy Grumman Boats, Marathon, New York

12

Serious White-Water Paddling

On a typical spring Sunday afternoon on western Pennsylvania's Youghiogheny River, a random passer-by might see a most curious sight—clusters of people lining the shore and peering towards a raft of canoeists stitched across the center of the river's rapids like a zipper gone slightly awry while a number of kayakers wait patiently to one side. If the passer-by was patient, he would soon see the canoeists peeling off one by one through the heady foam, paddling with desperate strokes, an occasional tipover mixing flailing arms and legs into the froth. A longer wait would produce an even more startling sight, a race in which overturned kayakers nonchalantly reappeared upright with paddle poised to continue on their way. Eventually, of course, our sightseer would realize he had happened upon a white-water canoe and kayak race.

Although both canoe and kayak have a North American pedigree, kayaking skills in particular have been advanced mainly by Europeans, chiefly Czechs and Germans. In fact, it was not until the summer of 1973 at Muotathal, Switzerland, that a U.S. competitive team captured a gold and silver medal—the first ever won by an American entry in wild-water and slalom world championships. In fact, for the first half of this century, a folding boat (kayak) invented by the Germans was practically alone on American white waterways. And even today, though the folding boat has given way to rigid reinforced plastic boats and other advances in white-water racing and boat making have been made, many of the designs seen on U.S. white water are pirated from abroad.

Today's white-water canoe also has its roots in Europe. These boats are decked and possess a more longitudinal curvature ("rocker"—see Chapter 2) in the keel than is usual in canoes, for better maneuverability.

Though the distinctions between kayak and canoe seem clear to someone looking at the two crafts at the same time, differences are not always so easy to describe. It is not true, for instance, that all crafts with covered decks are kayaks; canoes are sometimes equipped with coverings or rigid decks, too. On the other hand, kayaks and canoes do have different hull designs; for instance, the ends of a kayak are lower than the center as opposed to the canoe, in which the ends are higher than the center. And kayakers perch 1 to 3 inches above the bottom of the boat with their legs in front of them, while canoe paddlers kneel on the bottom and rest their hips on a thwart 6 to 10 inches above. Also, the kayak is always propelled by a paddle with a blade at both ends (positioned at right angles to each other to avoid wind resistance by the blade out of water), whereas canoeists wield a one-bladed paddle with a grip.

However, with the distinctions clear, it is nonetheless true that both canoes and kayaks have a place in the white-water competition limelight.

RACES

There are two kinds of white-water races—wild-water races

and the slalom. Wild-water or downriver events test the paddler's ability to get from a starting point to a finish line several miles distant in the shortest possible time. The object of the slalom, on the other hand, is to maneuver around a short course mapped through a rapids and punctuated with "gates" strung over the river on wires—an exercise which requires precise handling skills. Not only is course completion a race requirement but bumping a gate adds a penalty to the score.

In general, slalom craft are designed with shortest possible length, generous rocker, and softly curving cross sections, while

Slalom racer negotiating a gate. (Courtesy Old Town Canoe Company, Old Town, Maine)

wild-water craft have virtually no rocker, exaggeratedly curved cross sections, and greatest length possible in order to achieve the greatest speed.

Kayaks, with their narrow hulls and double-bladed paddles, are faster in wild-water racing, but the canoe can compensate for lack of speed in the slalom with its better maneuverability. However, kayaks and canoes are seldom pitted against each other in formal races.

THE ESKIMO ROLL

Kayakers—and occasionally canoeists, too—add an unexpected element to their races with the Eskimo roll, a spectacularly tricky maneuver used to right an overturned craft.

The Eskimo roll is employed when bracing strokes fail or the boat capsizes. The maneuver demands that its practitioner have no fear of water or failure. (The frequent failures accompanying the learning process will force the kayaker to exit his craft frequently underwater.)

There are more than two dozen ways to peform this maneuver (with or without a paddle, for example, or with one hand tied behind one's back). However, the important thing to remember is to reach the active blade of the paddle horizontally away from the hull, as far to the left as is possible (in a right-hand roll), turning the body from the waist toward that side. This begins the recovery stroke, which should be one smooth motion, the active blade sculling close to the surface in a backward arc as you pry yourself up at the other end of the paddle. At the surface, resist the temptation to immediately raise your body; roll your hips to right the boat, then follow with the body or you may tip over again. Don't forget to protect your head with a good lightweight helmet, available from most sporting goods stores.

Literally hundreds of canoe and kayak races take place in the United States. Many of them are sponsored by communities, clubs, park districts, chambers of commerce and other civic

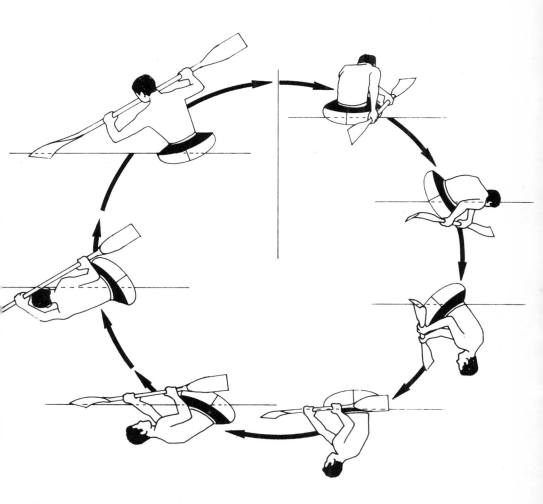

Figure 29.
The Eskimo roll.

The Eskimo roll. (Courtesy Old Town Canoe Company, Old Town, Maine)

organizations. However, for more information on the formal races—both on flat water and white water—held in this country and Canada, contact the following organizations:

In the United States:

American Canoe Association, 4260 East Evans Avenue, Denver, Colorado 80222

American Whitewater Affiliation, P.O. Box 1584, San Bruno, California 94066

U.S. Canoe Association, c/o Jack Snarr, 2316 Prospect Avenue, Evanston, Illinois 60201

In Canada:

The Canadian Canoe Association, 333 River Road, Vanier, Ontario, Canada (Telephone: 613-746-5455)

Appendix

Ten Regional Canoe Trips

NEW ENGLAND

The Saco River in Maine offers about 115 miles of excellent canoeing for families and beginners. From its source in the White Mountains of New Hampshire, the Saco winds eastward. The stretch from Fryeburg Center, Maine, to the bridge at East Brownfield is ideal for a weekend family canoe trip. However, trips of varying lengths are possible, due to the frequency of access at bridge crossings. There are also good swimming holes and sand bars ideal for camping. White-water runs occur at North Conway and Hiram. Take I-95 to the Westbrook exit, Route 302 to Bridgeton and Fryeburg, and turn north on Route 5 to the bridge at Fryeburg Center.

THE MID-ATLANTIC REGION

The Youghiogheny River, Pennsylvania, could be your introduction to white-water paddling. While much of the river is

Facing page courtesy Old Town Canoe Company, Old Town, Maine.

challenging, with swirling rapids rated up to Grade V, there is an 11-mile stretch of Grade II water between Confluence and Ohiopyle. There, with proper instruction, paddlers whose skills range from beginner to intermediate can practice their maneuvers. The "Yock" is one of the most popular rivers in the East, busy all season long.

For an exciting change of pace, try a raft trip out of Ohiopyle. In this do-it-yourself adventure, passengers are given necessary equipment and instruction.

THE SOUTH

The Withlacoochee River, Georgia/Florida, flows through the South's most picturesque swamplands, past sandy beaches and sentinel-like limestone buttes which were pitted by swirling currents eons ago. The river bends frequently, but the course is easy to find. However, there are numerous rapids and sometimes high waves. The Withlacoochee is high and swift during rainy seasons (March-May), but during normal dry periods (August-September), it may become necessary to portage over sand bars and around rapids. Put in where the river meets Georgia's SR-94 northwest of Valdosta. Take out 56 miles downstream at Suwannee River State Park, Florida, 12 miles south of Blue Springs.

THE MIDWEST

The Tittabawassee River in Michigan has a name more difficult to pronounce than the river is to paddle. In fact, this river offers easy canoeing with short portages around Secord and Smallwood dams. Put in on the upper reaches of either the main stream or the east branch about 15 miles northeast of Gladwin near the Ogemaw County line. There are several campsites in this wild, scenic country, and, in the quiet waters, fishermen will find bass, pike, and pan fish. The 30-mile paddle in Michigan's northern lower peninsula is good for a one- or two-day outing. Take out at Wixom Lake or Edenville Dam.

The Mackinaw River in Illinois, one of the most natural and un-spoiled rivers in the state, is fairly fast below Route 150 and free of obstructions except for a few submerged logs near the banks. The banks of the stream are low and the fields are cultivated to the water's edge. There are occasional sand bars, which in-crease in number as the stream cuts through the Illinois Sand Prairie bordering the Illinois River. Below Route 9 (the town of Mackinaw on Route 9 is about 3 miles from the river), where the best canoeing is found, the trees narrow to a thin border. There is a bridge between Route 9 and Route 121 at the blacktop road which runs due west from Bloomington and Route 9 south of Danvers. The river banks are high and there are occasional fallen trees, but wildlife is abundant on this pleasant, exciting stretch of the river. Put in at Mackinaw for 60 miles of good paddling to the Illinois River. Good fishing for catfish, carp, and smallmouth bass.

The Big Fork in Minnesota is a river for any paddler's schedule—whether he wishes to canoe for an afternoon or two weeks. Extending from the land of the Chippewas at Rainy River, Minnesota's Big Fork offers 220 miles of north-woods water. Tall pines and white birch line its banks, offering shelter to blue-winged teal, and the angler will soon fill his stringer with walleye. There are a few rapids at the start, but the section between Highway 6 and Bigfork is tame. North of Bigfork, however, the river becomes more turbulent and primitive, with two waterfalls that must be portaged; several exciting rapids challenge white-water skills.

THE OZARKS

The Buffalo River in Arkansas is a wild, free-flowing mountain stream in the northwestern part of the state that will go down as a success story in the annals of conservation. Forever preserved as a national waterway after an 11-year struggle by environmentalists, it is, in the upper reaches, a rugged river, a test of white-water skills. It is extremely popular during spring and early summer for float trips. The stretch between Buffalo State Park and White River is navigable throughout the year. The 7-mile stretch between Big Creek and Mt. Hershey has a good current and makes a pleasant outing.

The charm of the Buffalo is not limited to its swift-running channel. One may find abandoned cabins, scenic bluffs, and short, tranquil stretches that boast gravel bars where youngsters will delight in wading and hunting for souvenir pebbles.

THE NORTHWEST

The Columbia River, Washington, is typical of most Washington rivers—rugged and, in general, for the dauntless only. However, this famed river, the state's major inland waterway, does contain some navigable, scenic segments of flat water. Among these is a 13-mile stretch between Wanapum Dam and Priest Rapids Dam; this pleasant water trail provides a leisurely cruise past an old Indian settlement and Sentinel Gap, of interest to historians as a site where Indians once fished for the highly prized Columbia River salmon. One note of caution: High winds occasionally produce rough waves.

THE WEST

The Russian River, California, may get low in places during late summer and early fall, but it continues to enjoy great year-round popularity. With easy access from the San Francisco area, the river offers about 80 miles of canoeing and a diversity of trips, from pleasant half-day paddles between willow-lined banks to cruises of a week or more. There are canoe rental liveries (a large one at Healdsburg) and many short runs suited to beginners (the 27-mile stretch from Healdsburg to Reins

Beach, for example). Attractions include blackberry picking in June, steelhead fishing (during winter months), good swimming, and wildlife that includes turtles and green heron.

THE SOUTHWEST

The Angelina River in Texas offers a year-round, 14-mile trip through serene forests of pine and cypress between the Sam Rayburn Reservoir dam and Bevelport. Eminently suited to beginners, the gently winding emerald green river teems with black bass, crappie, and catfish. Controlled by the release of water through the dam, the current meanders along at a predictable 1 or 2 miles per hour. If you want to shorten the run to 7 miles, put in or take out at the Highway 63 bridge where there is a sloping bank of Bermuda grass. Good campsites dot the banks of the river, but they are all on private land, and canoeists should be sure to obtain permission before pitching their tents.